Excitement, drama, thrills, tears, and laughter in a book about a saint? The longer you read this amazing account, the closer you will feel to the very beginning days of the Christian church. The scandalous saint will become the man you would give anything to meet. In his heart lie secrets of how to release the unlimited power of God. When you have reached the last page, you will agree with me that when John Eils prays, God moves.

—*Merlin R. Carothers*
Founder, Foundation of Praise
Escondido, California

SCANDALOUS
SAINT

JOHN HAGEE

WHITAKER
HOUSE

SCANDALOUS SAINT

ISBN: 978-1-62911-001-1
Printed in the United States of America
© 1974, 2014 by Whitaker House

Whitaker House
1030 Hunt Valley Circle
New Kensington, PA 15068
www.whitakerhouse.com

1 2 3 4 5 6 7 8 9 10 11 **ʬ** 22 21 20 19 18 17 16 15 14

This book is lovingly dedicated to the memory of
Rosalinda Castro.

"He who gives a book gives more than cloth, paper, and
ink—more than leather, parchment, and words. He reveals a
foreword of his thoughts, a dedication of his friendship, a page
of his presence, a chapter of himself, and an index of his love."
—Unknown

ACKNOWLEDGMENTS

The harvest of happiness is most often reaped by the hands of helpfulness. For the many faithful friends who have helped bring this book into print, I wish to express my deep appreciation.

Joyce Jones typed and retyped the manuscript to produce a final product worthy of the missionary ministry of John and Josie Eils.

Frank Sepulveda's delightful *quinta* in Sabinas, Mexico, served as a quiet sanctuary where the complete outline and initial chapters were written.

My eternal gratitude to each one of you.

—*John Hagee*

CONTENTS

Though this book was first published in 1974, John and Josie Eils' story of radical faith and obedience is still an encouragement and challenge to believers today. In a time without modern-day technology, they fully relied on God's providence and sovereignty—a reminder that nothing can take the place of daily personal fellowship with the divine Pilot.

FOREWORD

It was during the night service of a summer youth camp in Indiana where I was showing slides of my father's missionary enterprise in Japan that I saw him. As my eyes traveled back and forth across that assembly of teenagers, they were drawn again and again to one that face located halfway back to my left—a face gripped in the throes of a destiny-making decision. It was the face of John Eils.

Five years later, John enrolled in International Bible College. As a student, he again stood out—always punctual, studious, athletic, and honest—but above all, uniquely zealous. I shall never forget his "missionary jug": a gallon jar he carried around constantly, with which he proceeded to relieve everyone around him of pocket change with his irresistible smile. Long before he joined the front ranks, he was backing the attack!

In my memory, John again stands out as one who wasted no time getting into the battle. With graduation behind him, he and his dedicated, charming wife, Josie, set out for Mexico. The details of what followed after their first time crossing the border constitute an action-packed drama that never fails to hold our student body and staff spellbound.

My father, Leonard Coote, IBC's founder, always used to say, "Impossibilities become challenges." No graduate of IBC has demonstrated that spirit more fully than John Eils.

—*David Coote* (1992–2012)
Former President, International Bible College
San Antonio, Texas

ONE

BOMBING RAIDS

The music of the finely tuned aircraft engine produced a comforting serenade for missionary pilot John Eils. At 4,000 feet, a few white clouds just below the plane looked like mountains of cotton. Above them, the dazzling blue skies stretched to the horizon, meeting the lush green carpet of the jungle.

Seated behind the pilot, staring at the magnificent handiwork of God, was the owner of the plane: John's twenty-one-year-old missionary friend and colleague, Jerry Witt. They had met in San Antonio years before, while John was attending International Bible College. Now Jerry was living in Mexico with his missionary father, who was stationed at Durango. Jerry and John were skilled pilots, having cut their teeth flying over rugged mountain terrain deep in Mexico's interior.

"There's the village on our bombing chart!" John's voice boomed above the engine noise in the tiny cockpit of the Piper Super Cruiser. Jerry glanced to his right, toward the village that was visible just off the tilted wing. Today was a great day for flying, and for bombing.

To achieve success, bombing raids must be planned beforehand to absolute perfection. The missiles that were used weren't lethal bombs that destroyed and mangled human bodies; they were gospels of John, written in the native tongue—a tremendously effective tool for getting the good news to remote villages in Mexico.

John checked the direction of the wind as Jerry positioned himself to drop the gospel bombs, each package carrying fifty booklets. They had to be dropped at precisely the right second so that they would land in the center of the village and not in the dense jungle.

The aqua-colored plane was losing altitude, floating down through the clouds like a mammoth bird looking for a place to settle. Jerry clutched the packages tightly, waiting for John's signal.

"Get ready!"

The plane was now sailing above the treetops, and the houses that had appeared as mere anthills from several thousand feet were rapidly becoming larger. The people of the village, who were invisible minutes before, now looked like scampering midgets. Those in the streets were waving their hands excitedly, while men in the plowed fields ran at breakneck speed, jumping the crooked rows, to get to their village. In a region where a radio is a treasured possession and a trip to town an annual event, an airplane buzzing overhead is one of life's biggest thrills.

At exactly the right moment, allowing for wind drift and altitude, John maneuvered the aircraft into an incredibly steep angle, so that one wing pointed toward God, while the other pointed toward the objects of His love.

"Now!"

At the staccato command, the gospels were dropped above the extended arms and hungry hearts of the excited villagers. As the booklets tumbled crazily through the air, tossing in the prop wash, the inhabitants scattered like center fielders, desperately trying to catch the precious gospels before they hit the ground.

John snapped the plane back so that the wings were level, then opened the throttle and raised the flaps. The view of the people and houses became smaller and smaller, eventually vanishing, as the plane burrowed into a thick mountain of fluffy white clouds.

Climbing 2,500 feet, the plane leveled off at its cruising altitude, and the missionaries exchanged satisfied smiles. The bombing raid had gone perfectly.

"Where to next?" Jerry asked.

It was customary on each bombing mission to drop gospels in as many villages as their supply would allow. But before John Eils could reply to the question, both men stiffened at the sound every pilot dreads.

The engine missed. The smooth rhythm changed all too quickly into rough sputtering. The propeller lost its hypnotic uniformity and began slashing the air with irregular bursts of frustration.

Both men, knowing the danger, stared in silence at the complex instruments and controls, almost begging for some clue as to why the plane was betraying them. The altimeter was spinning like a roulette wheel. The message was simple: they were approaching the ground—as well as death—at a rapid speed.

"Look for a place to land, Jerry! We're in trouble—real trouble!"

Both men scanned the terrain for a suitable place to make an emergency landing. The rugged mountains and deep canyons with their jagged rocks offered no consolation. Between the mountains were valleys filled with thick undergrowth and huge trees. Every indication from the ground spelled disaster.

"Lord, please help us!" John pleaded desperately. It was needless for either of the men to ask the other to pray; both had instinctively started praying the moment the engine had first sputtered. Both knew their breaths were numbered.

As the plane broke through the low clouds, the ground loomed before them. The trees were no longer green mounds on a lush green jungle carpet; they were harpoons of death drawing closer by the second.

"Look, John!" Jerry shouted, "There's an opening!"

John's eyes strained in the general direction of Jerry's pointed forefinger. It was an opening! But did they have enough altitude to make it that far?

Banking to the right, John nosed the plane through the air, using each precious inch of altitude to maneuver it ingeniously—something that years of missionary flying had taught him. The prop, unable to regain its rhythm, slashed sluggishly at the air as the engine sputtered a song of certain death.

"Jerry, that opening is not an ordinary one!" John exclaimed. "Looks like the dirt airstrip of some large ranch! If we can make it, we have a real chance."

Nodding his head in total agreement, Jerry licked his lips and tightened his seat belt. Neither said a word, but both knew that they were losing airspeed and altitude too fast; it was going to be close.

The branches of the trees reached upward as if trying to snatch the Super Cruiser from the air. The propeller stopped, and the engine died, but the strip was just over the next treetops. The frantic last-second efforts of the pilot carried the plane over the final tree as the wheels on the landing gear hacked through the branches. Both men braced themselves, breathed one last prayer, and waited for what seemed like inevitable death.

$\smile$

Josie Eils had never liked airplanes, and when her husband was flying, she found it impossible to relax until he phoned from the airport in Victoria to assure her he was safely on the ground again. John was always very thoughtful of her feelings, as she was of his. Tempted many times to ask him not to fly, she nevertheless refrained from doing so, knowing that it would be impossible for his ministry to succeed without the plane.

With it, he could take trips from village to village that otherwise would have required hours or days of travel by car during the rainy seasons. Even when it wasn't raining, the mountain roads were so treacherous and tortuous that to travel by car was both dangerous and agonizingly slow.

Josie glanced at the clock. John's call should have come long ago. To fight the nagging fear that attacked when she had to prolong her wait for the comforting ring of the phone and John's casual, Spanish-accented voice telling her that everything was fine, she had busied herself with household chores. Their German shepherd, Payaso,[1] trotted at her heels as she paced through the house, doing routine tasks to keep her mind occupied. When she had finished everything, she did it all a second time. Still no call.

John had never been so late calling before. Short flights were his self-imposed rule, because the mental alertness required for safe flying began to exhaust after about three hours. Flying in the mountains deep in Mexico's interior demanded constant concentration. Winds could change within seconds in the treacherous canyons. In addition, the jagged peaks and profound valleys caused updrafts and downdrafts that could smash a small plane to bits.

These factors were not a problem at high altitudes; but Josie knew that John and Jerry were flying at low altitudes over remote villages, dropping the precious gospels that the villagers cherished.

Having finished everything that needed to be done, Josie sat on the couch by the phone as if that would encourage it to ring. It

---

1. *Payaso* is the Spanish word for "clown."

didn't. John's call was now more than two hours late. Only prayer could conquer her rising panic. It would be dark soon—just how dark, she couldn't begin to know.

TWO

"VERY SERIOUS TROUBLE, SEÑOR"

The plane smashed violently on the dirt airstrip, and both missionaries fought to keep their faces from crashing through the windshield. It was only a matter of seconds, but it seemed like an eternity: the ripping of metal; the wild, uncontrollable skidding; the flying glass; the thick red dust that came sifting into the cockpit through gaping holes, making it almost impossible to breathe.

John's prevailing fear was that the small plane would flip over on its back, rupturing the gas tanks and causing an instant inferno. Even as the fear gripped his mind, the plane—skidding on its belly since its wheels had been torn off—was beginning to tip up on its nose. If it flipped over, they would burn before they could get out.

The propeller, twisted like taffy, was wrapped around the nose of the plane. The aircraft plowed down the rough airstrip with its tail in the air, its nose digging a furrow in the dusty earth. In a moment, the plane slid to a halt, balancing on its tip. It teetered for a few seconds in a vertical position.

The two men looked straight down at the ground and prayed that the plane wouldn't catch fire. In answer to their prayers, God's law of gravity summoned the shell of the plane to slam back to the earth with its precious cargo intact. There was no fire.

Quickly releasing their battle-tested seat belts, the two shaken missionaries eased themselves out of the cockpit, thrilled to be alive—and not even scratched.

They were faced with another crisis, however. The crash was sure to attract attention. It was possible that the authorities would see the gospels they carried and accuse them of distributing propaganda. (Although Mexican law states that the Word of God is not propaganda, local authorities make their own law.) Quickly, John and Jerry hid the gospels in a nearby ravine.

It was not a moment too soon, for they could hear the engine of an approaching truck. In a few moments, the truck stopped near the plane in a cloud of dust, and the driver cautiously got out. He introduced himself as the foreman of La Concepción Ranch. After he had satisfied his curiosity by closely examining the shattered plane, he motioned John and Jerry toward the truck, smiling mechanically and chattering incessantly about the terrible accident and how fortunate they were to be alive.

All the way to the ranch house, the stream of prater continued. John waited for the foreman to take a breath so he could ask a question, but it was in vain. The foreman seemed to breathe in the middle of his sentences, creating a never-ending stream of gabble.

"Where's the nearest town?" John finally broke in.

"Aldama!" the foreman replied. "You must come in and wash up and eat, since it is so near supper, and then we will go there."

John knew the Mexican people were very hospitable, and he was sure there was no need to be suspicious—but why did the foreman appear so nervous?

"I want to call my wife and let her know that we're all right," John told him.

"There's no telephone at the ranch," the foreman replied. "You will have to wait until later."

Seated at the table, waiting for the cook to serve supper, John heard what sounded like a telegraph key in operation. His feeling of uneasiness increased.

"Something's wrong, Jerry," John whispered. "The foreman is smiling too much and chattering too nervously."

The foreman had vanished. "Where is he now?" asked Jerry.

John shrugged his shoulders as his mind sought an explanation for the foreman's strange behavior.

After they had finished a delicious meal of frijoles and tortillas, the foreman returned, anxious to get going. It was already dark.

"Hurry, amigos, we must get to Aldama!"

John felt even more uneasy; when a Mexican starts to hurry, something very big is in the wind. But the missionaries had no choice but to accept the circumstances just as they were, and to hope that the foreman was merely excited over the spectacular crash.

On the way to Aldama, their rescuer's chatter mingled with the clatter of the truck. He asked a thousand questions but never waited for an answer. Suddenly, the monologue stopped, and the foreman began pumping the squeaky brake pedal.

"Why are we stopping?" John asked.

"Oh, I have to pick up someone here. They also need a ride into Aldama. You wait here, and I will go and get them."

He pulled the truck off the shadowy road onto a small dirt path that seemed to lead nowhere. He casually opened the door of the truck. As soon as his feet touched the ground, he slammed the door and sprinted into the thick darkness. John's suspicions were confirmed—something was up. But what?

"You're under arrest!" The words ripped through the darkness of the truck's cab with paralyzing suddenness. Both men froze, knowing they were in extreme danger. In the provincial areas of Mexico, the militant *rurales*[2] often take the law into their own hands. If a crime has been committed, the first suspect they encounter is often accused of being the culprit.

John and Jerry heard the cold sound of clicking steel as a moonlit reflection of a polished rifle barrel appeared in the truck's window. Holding the rifle was a police officer. They heard three additional clicks, and then they were surrounded by numerous riflemen eager to execute the orders of their *comandante*.[3]

"Why are we under arrest?" John wrestled to maintain his composure. If the Mexican comandante could smell fear, he knew they had it!

"You'll find out later. You are in very serious trouble, señor— very serious!" The comandante opened the door of the cab and ordered them to come out.

The ranch foreman stepped out of the darkness and apologized for his deception. "I'm sorry, señores. It's my duty to call the police when I see anything suspicious—and this looked very suspicious! While you were eating, I telegraphed the police from the ranch house and told them that you might be smugglers." He stepped back into the darkness behind the circle of rifles.

"We will spend the night in Aldama, amigos!" The voice of the comandante was sharp and shrill. He motioned his captives toward a battered Mercury—the official police car. "Get in and be careful!"

The warning was justified. The car didn't have a floorboard, and dust literally poured in as they sped toward the Aldama jail.

The following morning, it was decided that, because of the "seriousness of the crime" (which hadn't been formally named or even briefly discussed with the accused), the criminals must be taken to the magistrate in Tampico.

---

2. *rurales*: a colloquial term for a band of provincial police officers.

3. *comandante*: commander; leader.

The comandante who had arrested them chose one of his obese aides, Pedro Morales, to accompany him on the trip. The prisoners were escorted to another police vehicle—one that afforded the luxury of a floorboard. The officious rurales swaggered at every opportunity, for it was certain they had caught two smugglers worthy of crime's "Hall of Fame."

Their uniforms consisted of a shirt and pants of olive fabric, a hat of their own choosing, and large pistol. Morales was so convinced of the importance of these criminals that he carried a fully loaded M-1 rifle along with his pearl-handled pistols.

As the comandante motioned John and Jerry toward the police car, his pudgy aide scrambled for his rifle and gave them a guiding nudge toward the only vehicle in sight. He wanted everyone to know nothing was going to go wrong; a master criminologist was on the job, and his criminals were as good as in prison at that moment.

It was one hundred forty miles to Tampico, and their journey was uneventful until the comandante decided to stop and relieve himself. He left the car and stepped into the woods beside the road. Morales decided that, if this was to be the order of the day, he would join his comandante. He exited on the opposite side of the car so that the criminals would not have a route of escape. He forgot one minute detail, though; he left his loaded rifle in the front seat.

Waiting until the Sherlock Holmes of Mexico was well into the bushes, John lifted the rifle and shouted in the direction of the master criminologist in the weeds, "Hey, you left your rifle on the front seat—and it's loaded, amigo. It's loaded!"

Morales, obviously embarrassed, came scrambling from the bushes like an enraged bull elephant, grabbing at his pants and cursing as he staggered along.

"Leave that rifle alone, gringo!" He was screaming, his eyes bulging with fury.

John waited patiently for the man to regain his composure.

"If we were criminals, do you think you would be alive now?" he asked. "We're innocent of your smuggling charges, yet we're being treated as convicted criminals."

The comandante, who had returned hurriedly when he heard the uproar, gave his aide a withering look of scorn. They both got into the car. Morales dropped his head in shame and was silent the rest of the way to Tampico.

~

In Tampico, John and Jerry were brought before the magistrate who was to direct the interrogation. "Are you the pilots who crashed in a blue plane on La Concepción Ranch?"

Both missionaries hesitated.

"No, sir!" Jerry finally replied. "Our plane is greenish."

"Were you dropping propaganda from your plane?" asked the magistrate.

Both missionaries knew that the authorities had knowledge of the gospels, because, as the police had brought them into Tampico a few minutes before, they had seen a villager reading one. They also knew the penalty for distributing political propaganda in Mexico: a long prison term. Although Mexican law states that the Bible is not propaganda, they would not have a jury trial. The judge alone would determine whether they would be sent to prison and, if so, for how long.

Jerry chose his next words cautiously. "What do you mean by 'propaganda'?"

"Propaganda is propaganda. Were you dropping illegal literature?" the magistrate demanded, glaring at his hairsplitting defendants.

"No, sir," Jerry answered. "We were not."

"Take them to the next room!" ordered the magistrate.

Morales, still smarting from his roadside embarrassment, nudged his charges toward the room on their right. "Sit down," he commanded them.

The room was filled with photography equipment. Hanging from the wall was a series of numbers mounted on plaques—the type that are hung around the necks of convicted criminals for their mug shots. John could not resist the urge to grab one and drape it around his neck. Just as he put it on and smiled at Jerry, the photographer came in. He seemed upset by the facetiousness of these "criminals."

"You two hombres do not realize the very serious trouble you are in! There will be time enough for you to be photographed after you have been sentenced."

John returned the plaque to its proper place on the wall, reclaimed his seat beside Jerry, and waited for whatever was coming next. He still had not had an opportunity to call Josie; she must be frantic by now. His only choice was to wait.

In a few minutes, Morales walked in with his familiar M-1 rifle. Being at the capitol, surrounded by the high and mighty police force, must have helped him regain his self-respect.

"You are going to jail," he announced victoriously. "Follow me!"

They were led down a winding staircase into a dungeon measuring about fifty square feet. They stumbled along as they waited for their eyes to adjust to the dim lighting. The place smelled like an open sewer, and Jerry started dry-heaving at the stench.

Cells were arranged in a square around a central area of concrete that was occupied by a large barrel and a fat "white" pig that was nearly black with filth. The barrel was for the vomit of the drunks who could manage to reach it; the pig was there to clean up the residual matter of those who couldn't.

As they walked toward the door, a prisoner yelled in desperation, "You are Americans. I'm an American. Help me get out of this hellhole!"

The situation turned out to be most damaging.

The prisoner said he was from Amarillo, Texas, and that he had been imprisoned for smuggling. The aide seemed to enjoy their conversation. Circumstantial evidence holds great weight in the Mexican courts, and when Morales learned that Jerry was also from Amarillo, he rushed to his comandante with the news that the three prisoners had operated a smuggling ring with airplanes.

To prevent them from sharing their stories or plotting any ingenious attempts to escape from jail together, the authorities moved John and Jerry to a cheap hotel for an overnight stay, hoping there would be no mishaps in this very important case.

Relieved that they didn't have to spend much more time in the dungeon's stench, the missionary pair was marched out of jail and down the streets at gunpoint, having to endure the fascinated attention of the citizens. People scattered off the sidewalks and chattered excitedly about the two banditos who had been captured by the police. Morales' obnoxiously cocky swagger returned.

At sundown, they were marched into a hotel. The aide selected a room and led them through the narrow door.

"May I take a shower?" Jerry asked.

Pedro Morales gave this request grave consideration. After all, he might be plotting an escape. Then, reaching a delicate decision, he nodded his head up and down. Jerry stepped into the shower and pulled the curtain shut. Morales sprang to his feet and thundered, "No tricks! Keep the shower curtain open!"

"Tricks?" Jerry quizzed. "You've got the gun, and I'm here stark naked! What sort of trick do you think I could pull?" Waiting a moment before starting the shower, he could feel the aide's eyes on him. Morales gingerly placed the M-1 across his knees.

After showering, Jerry crawled into a stinking bed. The sway-backed mattress resembled a hammock. He suspected that the sheets had not been changed since the bed had last been used, earlier that day.

John did not have any more luck than Jerry. He showered, examined his bed, and bravely jumped in. He wasn't there for long. Within seconds, he shot out from between the sheets, yelling as if he'd been stabbed.

"What's the matter, señor?" inquired Morales, staring at John.

"Bedbugs!" replied John. "Bedbugs big enough to eat you alive!"

"You might as well get used to them, amigo. These bedbugs are nothing compared to the ones where you're going." The aide's face broke into an expansive smile. He propped himself up against the door, pushed his hat back on his head, and stared at his prisoners as if they might disappear into thin air. Since the room had no windows, the door was the only exit; yet he demanded that the light be left on. He bade his prisoners good night with another firm admonition not to try anything tricky.

John lay awake, his mind racing. What must Josie be thinking by now? If only he could call her! Maybe he would get a chance tomorrow. He would also call the American consul, identify himself as an American citizen, and ask for help.

Before he drifted to sleep, John thought of the apostle Peter's overnight stay in prison: *"Peter was sleeping between two soldiers, bound with two chains: and the keepers before the door kept the prison"* (Acts 12:6). Peter was delivered from prison by the prayers of the church members at home who refused to forget about him. John wondered if anyone was praying for him now. Was a long prison term in his future? What would happen to Josie and the churches they had started?

He remembered the covenant he and Josie had made with God en route to Mexico eight years earlier. With no financial support, they had entered Mexico as missionaries to present the glorious gospel of Jesus Christ. Both had agreed that it was a venture of naked faith in God's divine ability to provide for their every need in every situation. After all, had He not done it for the disciples in the New Testament?

Jesus told His followers to go *"into all the world, and preach the gospel"* (Mark 16:15). They were not told to establish church boards or organize committees to approve or disapprove of God's directives, or to worry about retirement plans or plush parsonages. Their only command was to "Go!"

Following the New Testament pattern, John and Josie had invaded Mexico, pledging to each other that when God quit supplying their needs, they would leave the mission field. God had met their need at every crisis. Staggering miracles had occurred.

Tonight, it looked as if the massive steel doors of one of Mexico's infamous prisons were going to clang shut behind John. As he remembered how God had so miraculously provided in times before, John was flooded with supernatural confidence that the Lord would come to his aid as He had before. And with that, he drifted off to sleep.

THREE

"WHAT WERE YOU SMUGGLING?"

The rays of the early-morning sun streamed through the doorway into the dingy hotel room, waking the missionaries. The aide had also slept for a while, although he would never admit it. It was seven o'clock, and he reminded the two "masters of crime" that they must be at police headquarters in one hour.

Both prisoners rolled out of bed. Their bodies were covered with welts—bedbug bites. Reluctantly, they put on their filthy clothes, which were saturated with the red dirt of the airstrip. After examining their pockets, they exchanged a shrug of the shoulders to acknowledge a circumstance to which they were very well accustomed—they were nearly broke. They were not expecting the luxury of breakfast, anyway.

The aide pointed his forefinger in the direction of the open door leading outside to the narrow dirt street. Perfunctorily obeying his gesture, both men found themselves in the streets of Tampico with an M-1 rifle pointed toward their backs. The local people seemed even more excited than the evening before. It was obvious that the prisoners had been the topic of conversation around many supper tables last night.

The morning air was fresh and crisp. The leaves of the trees glistened, and the heavy dew sparkled on the grass. Inspired by nature's beauty, John doubled his pace. Morales hung back a few feet, trying to catch his breath.

Above the clatter of the morning traffic—horse-drawn wagons, bicycles, and an occasional dilapidated car—rose the shrill voice of a newsboy. John froze in his tracks. The voice came again, echoing through the open plaza up ahead.

"Did you hear what he said?" John asked Jerry.

"I heard. I can't believe it. I just can't believe it!" Jerry replied.

When they crossed the street, John held up a peso and whistled. The paperboy ran toward them, announcing the headlines as he came: "'Smugglers Captured at La Concepción Ranch and Brought to Tampico for Trial!' Read it in my newspaper!"

John gave the newsboy a peso and waited for the correct change as Morales poked his back with the rifle. The newsboy began to fumble for change when he noticed the rifle and then studied his customer. His hands were suddenly paralyzed, and the color drained from his deep brown face. The picture in the paper—it was this man! A real bandito was right in front of him.

Realizing the newsboy was overcome with shock, John told him to keep the change; then they resumed their walk toward headquarters.

Regaining his voice and screaming in near hysterics at every passerby, the newsboy explained that the bandito in his paper was just up the street in front of the policeman with the big gun. In a matter of minutes, he sold every paper.

John persuaded Morales to let them stop long enough to read the article. They climbed up on an unattended shoeshine stand and quickly scanned the piece recounting their crash. Engrossed in his reading, John was unaware that the *bolero*[4] had started shining

---

4. *bolero*: a colloquial term used in Mexico to designate a "shoeshine boy."

his shoes. As he folded up the newspaper, he told the bolero that he had no money. The boy gasped in terror. Pointing his finger at the man he was certain was a public enemy, he shouted, "You're the gringo going to prison!" The bolero began backing up into the street, legs shaking, then looked over his shoulder and began yelling to his compadres that he had just shined the shoes of a great bandito.

Morales reminded his two charges that they had to be at police headquarters in ten minutes for interrogation.

John thought of Josie. What would she think if she heard the news? "May I please call my wife?" he asked in desperation.

The aide agreed, almost compassionately.

When they arrived at police headquarters, John phoned home while Morales' rifle rested between his shoulder blades.

"Hello?"

The sound of Josie's voice filled him with confidence. "Hi, Sunshine!" he greeted her.

"John—" Her voice seemed to break momentarily from the strain of worry. "Where are you? Where have you been? Why haven't you called?"

"One question at a time, Sunshine. I'm fine, and so is Jerry. We had to make an emergency landing on a ranch airstrip and have been captured by the authorities. We're at the police headquarters in Tampico. Could you bring us some clothes and money?"

"How much money, John?"

"All you can get your hands on. We've been charged with smuggling, and if the Lord doesn't come to our rescue, things could get very bad." John's voice communicated the tension of the past two days.

"I'll be there shortly. You have the keys to our car, so I'll have to ask Ernie McCullum to bring me." She waited for his approval.

"That'll be fine. I'll see you this afternoon—and remember, don't worry. Somehow, someway, God will help us work this out!"

"He always does," Josie replied. "I'm sure He will this time! Bye for now."

The phone clicked, and the sight of the M-1 rifle brought John back to his present dilemma: Would it be prison or pardon? He and Jerry walked in silence down a hallway toward a very uncertain destiny. It was unbelievable, yet it was happening—happening to them.

They were directed into an office where they were greeted by the smiling face of a polite magistrate. Following a very brief exchange of pleasantries, the interrogation began with a question of assumed guilt designed to shake the confidence of the accused. John knew he would be held responsible; Jerry was too young.

"What were you smuggling, Señor Eils?" The gaze of the magistrate was fastened on John. His eyes were so penetrating that John almost started to believe he was guilty.

"I wasn't smuggling, sir," John replied.

"Then what are you and your friend doing in Mexico?"

"We are here on tourist visas for six months."[5]

"Did you file a flight plan when you left Victoria?"

"Yes, sir."

After a few more questions, the magistrate stopped abruptly and left the room. Immediately, another group of interrogators entered and asked the same questions. That group was followed by another, and then another. The interrogation lasted three hours. The groups compared notes in the hall to see if the prisoners' story broke down.

---

5. Only Mexican citizens are permitted to stay in Mexico more than six months without reregistering with the Department of Immigration. All missionaries work on six-month tourist visas until they have been in Mexico long enough to apply for citizenship.

The magistrate reentered the room, smiling politely at the haggard suspects. He apologized mechanically for the inconvenience as he shuffled through some papers on his desk, searching for a specific item. When he found what he was looking for, he shoved the legal documents across the desk toward John.

"Sign these, please." His voice was pleasant—too pleasant. His forefinger marked the line awaiting John's signature.

The magistrate looked a bit surprised when John took the legal documents and began reading them. He hadn't let on that he was fluent in Spanish. The papers were in fact a complete confession that he was guilty of smuggling contraband into Mexico. The specific nature of the contraband was not mentioned. John stared at the magistrate's smiling face.

"Sir," his voice reverberated off the concrete walls, "this is a full confession of guilt. This is absolutely ridiculous! No, sir, I won't sign these papers. Furthermore, now that we've been charged, I'll contact the US Embassy and ask them to intercede for us."

"Fine, fine! I look forward to hearing from the consul in your behalf." The magistrate paused, crossing his arms over his chest and leaning back in an ancient swivel chair. Then he continued, "The aide will take you two across the street for lunch." He was still smiling broadly.

"Are we still under arrest?" John asked.

"You're in our custody and will remain so, amigos, until you are completely cleared of all charges."

The next morning, John repeatedly tried contacting the US Embassy by phone. The receptionist kept telling him that no one was in the office.

"C'mon, Jerry," John said as he hung up the phone for the last time. "We have to find help somewhere."

As they stepped out into the street, they were thrilled to see Josie walking toward them, accompanied by Ernie McCullum, a business friend from Victoria. John had given Josie the nickname "Sunshine" while they were courting, and today she lived up to her name; she was like bright sunshine on a dark, dark day.

After a prolonged hug and a short kiss between husband and wife, the four of them headed across the street to purchase a decent meal with some of the money Josie had brought. Morales followed closely behind, a bit troubled at having to guard a quartet instead of just two.

They spent over an hour catching up while enjoying the wonderful, spicy Mexican food. Then the aide informed them that lunch hour was over—and so was the visit. John and Josie said good-bye without having a clue as to what would follow. They had been in many difficult situations before, and the Lord had always delivered them. They were inwardly confident that He would rescue them this time, as well.

Josie and Ernie returned home to Victoria. Now that John had some money, he and Jerry decided to get a better room at Hotel Inglaterra. Tonight there would be no bedbugs. They would have a neatly decorated room with excellent accommodations, and enjoy a thorough cleaning for the first time since the crash. It had been a long week.

Sunday is a very special day in a missionary's life. It is a time to fellowship with native pastors and enjoy heartwarming services all day. It's a special treat to hear the residents sing worship songs. When Mexicans sing hymns, their faces seem to light up with a special radiance that reflects the redemptive work of Jesus Christ.

This Sunday, John and Jerry were not looking into the faces of the people they loved; they were looking down the black barrel of the rifle that had been pointed in their direction since shortly after the accident. They endured the day in custody, waiting for another round of interrogation the next morning. Only the Lord knew what was in store for them after that. The day dragged on—minute by minute—until the sun set over the horizon. They prayed they would never have to spend another day in such misery.

⌒

Monday finally arrived, and Morales escorted the two missionaries to the police headquarters. After a brief discussion, everyone was commanded to return to the crash site to look for contraband.

John and Jerry were hustled into a waiting police car as twenty green-clad soldiers jumped into a two-ton Chevy truck to follow and assist them in the search. At this point, John was convinced that the magistrate wanted to clear up two smuggling charges in one operation. Jerry, the other man from Amarillo had been charged with smuggling, as well; they were all Americans; they were all flying airplanes. Too many circumstances suggested they were connected. Only days before, he would have refused to believe that he could ever be found guilty on a charge of smuggling. Now, after the extensive interrogation, the newspaper headlines, the reactions of the townspeople, and the constant presence of the aide with his rifle, he wasn't too sure what was going to happen. If the gospels they'd transported were discovered, the comandante might arbitrarily classify the material as propaganda and sentence both him and Jerry to long prison terms.

When the procession pulled up in front of the general store located on the ranch, the truckload of young, aggressive soldiers and the magistrate's staff created more excitement than Pancho Villa and the Mexican Revolution, attracting spectators from under every rock. Through the swinging doors stepped the ranch foreman, beaming and shaking hands with every person in sight.

As the one who had captured these now-famous gringos, he was the hero, and everyone listened to him give a well-rehearsed, detailed account of the momentous event. John's fears were confirmed. He would no doubt have to tell the crowd that he and Jerry dropped gospels over the villages.

Bounding out of the police car, John headed for the ranch foreman, who suddenly fell silent when he saw the gringos he had turned over to the rural police under the pretense of helping them. He was stunned when John gave him a tremendous *abrazo*.[6]

Every eye narrowed in on them; all ears were listening intently. John seized control of the conversation in order to deter the foreman from making any mention of the gospels, which would almost assuredly send him and Jerry to prison.

With his arm still around the foreman's shoulders, John said, "This man is a true Mexican. Here we were, visiting your great country on a tourist visa, when we got lost in our airplane. Our engine suddenly quit, and we barely escaped with our lives. This man came from nowhere as an angel of mercy to save us."

Realizing that he had the attention of his audience, John continued his eulogy. "He gave us food and water and was so kind to inform the authorities that we were stranded here at La Concepción Ranch and needed help. This man, amigos, is a great, great Mexican!"

The ranch foreman was radiant. He proceeded to verify John's story, lavishing still more praise upon himself in the process. He never mentioned the gospels.

The magistrate was impressed with the magnificent oratory. "Everyone to the scene of the crash!" he demanded. "We must conduct an intensive investigation for our reports."

Dust gathered into a cloud as everyone scrambled to the crash scene. They went by horse, by bicycle, and on foot, trailing the police car and the Chevy truck full of soldiers. This was, without doubt, a great moment in the history of La Concepción Ranch.

---

6. *abrazo*: hug; embrace.

As soon as the police car stopped, John and Jerry were ordered out at gunpoint. They walked in the direction opposite the ravine where the gospels had been hidden, ostentatiously kicking up leaves with their feet, drawing everyone's attention to themselves. The masses followed as if attracted by a magnet. Every bush was searched; leaves were scattered in the search for clues; rocks were turned over; hollow trees were examined. Not a single gospel was discovered. The multitude roamed the area, waiting to find some great evidence to prove the prisoners guilty.

They found nothing. The disappointed magistrate ordered a suspension of the search, which seemed to end as quickly as it had begun. The military escort and police officers returned to Tampico.

John's hopes were rising, but he cautioned himself. Experience had taught him that nothing is ever settled in Mexico until it's completely over, and there were many things that could go wrong before he and Jerry were freed. Even while they had been at the crash site, someone might have harassed a confession out of the man from Amarillo, and altered it to include them. What if the man had signed it in ignorance, thinking it was a release?

John and Jerry reentered the office of the magistrate full of apprehension. Smiling broadly, the officer lifted his hands as if surrendering, and proclaimed, "You're free! Please sign these papers accepting responsibility for the aircraft and any damage to the airstrip."

The last legal documents John had read were a confession of guilt. And what was this? It was exactly what the magistrate had said. John signed it quickly as the feeling of freedom pushed the unbelievable nightmare into momentary oblivion.

As the two missionaries left the police headquarters in Tampico, John reflected that this was not his first experience with prisons.

"Lord," he said under his breath, "what is it with me and jails? Seems like I could do with a little less scandal!"

FOUR

"YOU ON THE THIRD ROW...."

For many years, Eva Newhouse worked tirelessly for the Salvation Army in Los Angeles, trying to lift the terrible burdens carried by her fellow men. On an October day in 1938, she went to fulfill a special assignment given to her from God. She had a feeling about her infant grandson, John Burnhardt Eils Jr., that surpassed human knowledge, and today she would take him to Angelus Temple and ask the famous evangelist Aimee Semple McPherson to dedicate him to the Lord.

Climbing the wide marble steps leading to the circular sanctuary, she held the infant close to protect him from the chilly wind. Once inside the temple, she took off his blankets and selected a seat in the front row.

As the service ended, she caught the attention of Sister Aimee. "I want you to dedicate this baby to the Lord!" she said. She didn't want to share her secret feelings, though. Perhaps God would confirm them with the words Sister Aimee would utter in the precious moments of his dedication.

Taking the child in her arms, the evangelist began praying with obvious anointing. "Lord, take this child and use him in Your ministry...." The prayer continued, confirming that this baby had a very special future.

Wiping tears of joy from her eyes, Eva carried the blessed boy, shrouded in divine glory, from Angelus Temple. She did not know what a "scandalous saint" her grandson would become, but she was sure that he had been sealed for God's service.

Four years later, the child Sister Aimee had dedicated spent his first night in jail. Following a controversial divorce, his father had kidnapped him from his home under the pretense of taking him for a short ride on his motorcycle. The motorcycle ride had carried them from Los Angeles to the small town of Kenosha, Wisconsin, where John Eils Sr. had run out of money. He had asked if he and his son could spend the night in jail, and permission had been granted.

A newspaper reporter who had learned of the situation came and took their picture the following morning before they left. That night, the front page of the evening paper featured the photograph of the four-year-old inmate and his father.

Responding to the demands of the law, John's father returned to Los Angeles to acquire full legal custody of the "little jailbird." After the legal battle had been settled, he returned to Kenosha, Wisconsin, and opened a jewelry shop. He was a skilled watch repairman, and his business prospered. He soon began dreaming aloud of the day when his talented son would join him in the business. He was already making the preparations for John to study under the supervision of one of the nation's finest and most ingenious engravers. When John Jr. had completed his training, they would open a shop and repair watches and engrave trophies, plaques, jewelry, souvenirs, and other objects. A financial bonanza was certain.

However, he failed to recognize his son's rare commitment to the church and to Sunday school. While most children needed to be encouraged, if not bribed, to attend Sunday school, John always waited eagerly for the church bus to come by his house to take him to Lake Shore Tabernacle, where God's perfect will for his life continually unfolded before him.

At ten years of age, John was sitting near the back of the church when God unveiled to him His interest in his life. The guest speaker walked straight up to him and uttered words that, for a moment, seemed generic: "Thus saith the Lord: If you will keep your mind, your lips, and your hands clean, I will use you to bless other men." Though the prophetic statement might have sounded like a platitude to the congregation of hundreds, it had a lasting effect upon John. When he was tempted to swear, he remembered the utterance and refused to defile his lips. When urged to smoke in adolescence, he refused to do so. While his peers reveled in filthy conversation and lewd jokes, those things "turned him off." Just how he might bless other men, he didn't know; but he was determined to obey God's instructions.

It was some time later, however, when he realized that mere obedience would never do. He needed a personal Savior. When he realized this, he opened his heart to Jesus Christ and became a born-again Christian.

Three years after he received the prophecy at church, John began making plans to attend a youth function at Camp Krietenstein near Brazil, Indiana. That youth camp was not to be just another joyous, youthful excursion. It was to be an opportunity for God to show him that He was guiding him step-by-step. Two events occurred on the trip that assured him he was God's property forever.

One event occurred on the first night. A man came up to him after the service, laid his hands on his forehead, and calmly spoke these words: "Thus saith the Lord: If you will keep your mind, your lips, and your hands clean, I will use you to bless other men." It was difficult for John to contain his joy at the moving of the Holy Spirit within him; this man had repeated verbatim the prophecy that had been spoken over him three years before. He never saw the man again—but he knew God must have had, from the very beginning, an important assignment for him.

Thinking it impossible that God could bless him much more in one short week, John settled back to enjoy the fun and fellowship of the camp. There were exciting Bible studies in the morning, recreation in the afternoon, and evening worship services that were memorials of God's grace. Yet these times of fellowship were only the beginning of his walk with God.

David Coote, then president of International Bible College in San Antonio, Texas, was the featured speaker at the camp. Earlier that year, while touring Kyoto, Japan, he had been strangely attracted to Sanjusangendo Hall, a Buddhist temple. Inside the temple had been images of 1,001 Buddhas, each with thirty-three pairs of arms and thirty-three sets of wings. Steadying himself against a marble pillar, David Coote had taken a photo with an Argus C-3 camera, which he had never used in such poor light. By God's providence, the colored slide had developed perfectly.

Months later, at the Krietenstein Youth Camp, he showed this picture to young people from all sections of America. It had a special meaning for one thirteen-year-old boy from a broken home. As Coote flashed the picture on the screen, he made a simple statement that would lead John Eils to surrender his life to Christ and become a missionary of the gospel: "The gods in this temple have more than 66,000 arms, yet they are powerless to help even one lost heathen. They have more than 66,000 wings, yet they are powerless to rescue even one perishing soul!"

The picture changed, but the image was burned into John Eils' heart forever. To this day, when circumstances are bitter and harsh, John remembers that picture and gains assurance from the knowledge that he serves a God whose arms are not shortened and whose ears are always listening to His children's cries. (See Isaiah 59:1.)

⌒

It was upon his return home from the youth camp that John learned something else that impressed him very deeply: God cares very much about the sicknesses of mankind and is eager to heal His children. From his earliest years, John had suffered from extreme sinus blockages. He was bedfast with every attack. Even at his best, he could seldom breathe through his nose, and at night, his snoring announced his condition to everyone else in the house.

All his life, John had heard about divine healing. His father, who at one time had been preparing for the ministry, had been in a motorcycle accident that had pulverized his ankle. The most talented surgeon had refused to touch the ugly mass of tissue and had pronounced it utterly hopeless. John Eils Sr. had been told by the doctors that he would never walk again.

But he had attended a healing service at Angelus Temple and, after prayer, had taken off his cast to reveal a completely healed leg. John Jr. didn't understand why his father hadn't followed through with his intentions to become a minister, especially after he'd experienced such a miracle.

Along with this miracle, John also remembered the young people at the youth camp who had testified that God had healed them—and many of their testimonies had been verified by medical experts.

John made up his mind that it was senseless for him to suffer with this horrible, throbbing sinus problem when he served a God of miracles.

The first revival that came to Lake Shore Tabernacle found his faith in orbit. He announced to his stepmother, whom he loved dearly, "I'm going to be healed of my sinus trouble tonight—and I'll never suffer another day with it."

His stepmother laughed. She didn't attend church very often and had no faith in divine healing. She patted John's blond head affectionately and said, "We'll see, John. Don't get too excited about it!"

It was customary at his church to have a healing service after the main service, should anyone express a desire for it. John could hardly wait for the main service to end. It seemed to drag on.

At the close of the service, the preacher asked, "Would anyone like prayer for healing tonight?"

This was John's moment. He uncoiled from his seat like a tense spring and was the first to reach the altar. Others approached more casually, and it was an exercise in patience for him to wait for them. He just knew that when the preacher finished praying, his nose and sinuses would be opened, and he would be able to breathe freely for the very first time in his life.

The minister anointed him with oil, as the book of James instructs, and began to pray. John tarried for a moment after the prayer, waiting for the manifestation of his healing. Nothing happened—absolutely nothing!

Dejectedly, he walked to the rear of the church and entered the restroom, where he blew his nose so vigorously that his ears popped and whistled. No results. He waited a few minutes, thinking that maybe God needed a little time. Still nothing!

Returning to his seat three rows from the front, he sat down beside his lifelong friend Duane McCormick. Still experiencing utter disappointment, he said nothing; mercifully, his friend asked him nothing. Maybe his stepmother had been right; maybe he shouldn't have gotten too excited about all this healing business.

The booming voice of the preacher snatched him from his private thoughts: "Son, you in the third row with the blond hair—stand up and praise the Lord! He healed you tonight!"

John was in the spotlight. If he stood and said, "I'm healed," he would be lying—and he was known for his truthfulness. If he stood and said, "I'm not healed," he would be calling the minister a liar before the entire congregation. What should he do?

To his own amazement, he found himself getting to his feet and heard his voice uttering the words, "I believe that Jesus Christ heals, and by faith I claim my healing!" Immediately, an intense, penetrating heat struck him between the eyes, and he began to stagger as if he were about to faint.

In a matter of seconds, the burning sensation lifted—and so did his lifelong sinus problem. Fresh air came pouring through his nose for the first time in months. It was like the breath of heaven itself. He could hardly contain his excitement; God had healed him—really healed him! He wondered what his stepmother would say to all this.

Bounding through the door of his home after the service, he announced joyfully, "I was healed tonight! I was healed tonight!"

"Big deal," his stepmother replied unenthusiastically. "We'll see how you get along tonight."

At two in the morning, John was awakened by his stepmother shaking his shoulder. "Blow through your nose, John," she insisted. Obediently, he then inhaled, filling his lungs, and exhaled two streams of air through his nostrils.

His stepmother was amazed but remained unconvinced. Every night for the next two weeks, she would come to his bedroom and demand that he breathe through his nose. His sinuses remained open, as they do even to this day.

John was so excited about his healing that knew he could never turn back. He wanted all that God would give him. Small wonder, then, that he was soon baptized in the Holy Spirit—an experience that proved to be a great blessing in his Christian walk.

The next year, his father moved the watch shop back to California. He still hoped his son would join him in the business, and often talked of the financial bonanza they would discover as a watch-repair team. But John had other ideas in mind.

Four years later, he told his father he wanted to enroll at International Bible College to study missionary work. In a voice that shook with emotion, his father replied, "If you go to Bible college, John, you'll get no help from me! You'll have to get a job and pay your own way."

From that time on, John's father hardly spoke to him. For a while, John's heart throbbed with grief—but he served the Healer of broken hearts. A Scripture that often came to his aid was Psalm 27:10: *"When my father and my mother forsake me, then the LORD will take me up."*

John was in a spiritual valley where the shadows were as dark as the night. He loved his father dearly and refused to hold bitterness toward him, but he couldn't understand why he'd reacted the way he had.

God had encouraged John thus far by means of two identical prophecies, a heathen picture that burned in his brain, and an undeniable healing. God was with him—he knew it by faith, even though certain circumstances seemed to suggest otherwise.

On the day after his father's refusal to help send him to Bible college, he began searching for a job—any job. But his search was fruitless.

Although John's most pressing need was for a job to pay for his education, he also felt an equal urgency to study the Bible. He felt very confused about what God wanted him to do.

"*No good thing will he withhold from them that walk uprightly.*" That was God's promise in Psalm 84:11. Before going to bed that night, John wept before God as he claimed that verse in his crisis.

The next morning, he was prompted by the Holy Spirit to apply for a job as a lifeguard. He was qualified, having been a medalist swimmer in high school. He first went to the Playa del Rey. Spotting a man who appeared to be in charge, he approached him, mentally rehearsing all the lines he had used the day before.

"I'm looking for a job…" He paused. "Would you possibly have any openings here?"

The man behind the desk looked him over. "Yes, we do. Can you work this afternoon?"

After all the failures of the day before, John was thunderstruck. By simply taking God at His word, he was hired at the first place he stopped, in less than one minute! Had he known where he was to be assigned, he would have understood that God was going to supply not only his needs but also the desires of his heart. John had wanted a place to be alone, and he was about to get one that paid $1.85 per hour.

Ninety-six lifeguards made up the Los Angeles Beach Division, and each had a particular section of the beach to supervise. When John walked to his assigned section after lunch, he could hardly believe his eyes. There were signs posted everywhere that said, "Positively No Swimming. Dangerous Riptides." He walked to his lifeguard stand, climbed into the chair, and imperiously ordered a lone seagull to stay out of the water.

Ninety-five lifeguards were laughing at him and his ridiculous assignment, but John was praising the Lord. The next day, he went to his deserted section of the beach with his Bible and banjo in hand. For three months, he spent most of each day feasting on the Word of God and singing to the seagulls.

At the end of the summer of 1955, John had earned enough money to pay for his first semester at International Bible College. His boss was so pleased with his attitude that he promised him a job the following year if he chose to come back.

During the summer, the other guards had come to realize that there was something different about this happy lifeguard; therefore, they all took time to come by and wish him well on his last day. Even though his father had not seen the same spark, he agreed to drop John off at the bus station. John's single suitcase held all of his belongings, and there was still room for the contents to rattle around. As he stepped onto the bus for Texas, he knew that he was fulfilling the will of God for his life. Sixteen hundred miles away was a tiny evangelical Bible college where he would find a God so big that no scandal or heartbreaking circumstance in the years to come could defeat him.

FIVE

INTERNATIONAL BIBLE COLLEGE

Twenty-seven hours and 1,800 miles later, the Greyhound bus zipped past the San Antonio city line. A weary missionary-to-be tumbled off downtown at Central Station, stretched his cramped legs, raised his aching arms high into the air, and promised himself it would be a while before he took another long bus ride.

Inside the terminal, he ate a quick snack while looking at a city map stapled to the wall. Locating International Bible College, he marked the spot with his forefinger, made a mental note of the address, and reluctantly boarded a worn-looking city bus that would take him there.

The day was sultry; a neon temperature sign on the bank read 102 degrees. The sweltering streets were gorged with sweaty people, but John was hardly aware of his surroundings. His mind was too preoccupied with speculations about his immediate and very uncertain future. What did it hold?

He tried to imagine what the small evangelical campus would look like: magnificent, with towering brick buildings adorned with ivy, lush green grass, shaded paths, fraternity houses, and gobs of young people excitedly preparing for their future life.

But when he arrived at the IBC campus, a battered suitcase in hand, his mouth fell open in utter amazement. Before him were several reconditioned army barracks scattered over ten acres of sun-bleached Texas limestone. At the center of the campus stood a two-story building of pale yellow stucco, which, he would learn, served as an administration building and cafeteria. San Antonio was in the final stage of a seven-year drought. The mis-shapen leaves on the trees were withered and curled, their color an ugly brown; the grass looked as if it had been last watered by Moses. There were no ivy-shrouded brick cathedrals of learn-ing—only asbestos-covered barracks; no shaded paths—just one large gravel drive arcing through the campus like a fallen rain-bow. At the moment, he wouldn't have believed that this forlorn piece of real estate was lovingly known around the world by its devoted graduates as "Hallelujah Hill." It would soon become a cherished citadel of inspiration to him, but today it looked like a hot Siberia.

John dragged his feet along the dusty, crushed-gravel path leading to the aging administration building. He hadn't walked fifty feet, however, before his disappointment turned to surprise. Standing on the steps of the building was Lennie Block, a friend from his home church in Kenosha, Wisconsin. They hadn't seen each other in four years.

"Lennie!"

The figure on the steps turned in the direction of John's joyful shout. All doubt was instantly removed as the long-separated friends approached each other and exchanged an affectionate embrace.

"John Eils! What are you doing at IBC?" Lennie asked.

The next hour passed quickly as John excitedly recounted the events that had brought him to this place for missionary minis-try. Within the hour, he met two more friends from the church in

Kenosha: Duane McCormick and Madeline Scott. His heart was full of joyful exultation.

Walking toward the transformed barracks, he was no longer aware that the grass was dead. He knew only that he could hardly wait for classes to start. He and Lennie had agreed to be roommates, and they were going to search together for a room in the barracks.

"Have you had a chance to look for a job?" John asked as they entered the two-story dorm.

"Yes, and this town is tough—real tough!" Lennie said. "The pay scale is low because the abundance of Mexican-American labor. Students are more than willing to take jobs for fifty-five cents an hour."

"Fifty-five cents an hour?" John closed his eyes and grimaced. Such a wage was unthinkable. He fought down rising panic as his father's words sounded like kettledrums in his ears: *"No help, no help, no help!"*

The two located a vacant room and claimed it as their own. It was clean, spacious, and Spartan. The simple furnishings consisted of two metal cots and a couple of small wooden tables. John remembered the words the apostle Paul had written to his friends in Philippi: *"For I have learned, in whatsoever state I am, therewith to be content"* (Philippians 4:11). As he unpacked his meager belongings from a suitcase that looked as if it was ready to self-destruct, John revived the conversation on employment. "I left a job in California making a dollar eighty-five an hour supervising stray seagulls. Now I am faced with the magnificent pay scale of fifty-five cents an hour. It's unbelievable—absolutely unreal!"

"Correction, John," Lennie said. "That's only if you can find a job. Have you ever considered washing dishes?"

"No way, pal." John's tone revealed his adamance. "If there is one thing I detest, it's washing dishes. That's out—definitely out."

John's search for employment that afternoon was drier than the local drought. That was two weeks before he struck water— dishwater! The college gave him a work grant and assigned him the prestigious job of head dishwasher, at a salary of fifty cents an hour. He served in that noble capacity for three years, earning supplemental money mowing lawns after classes. But through it all, he learned a valuable lesson: Happiness comes not from having much to live on but having much to live for.

His most pressing need having been met, John began to give some thought to other considerations. One Friday afternoon, he initiated a conversation with Lennie about something of interest to most eighteen-year-old boys.

"Lennie, how do you go about dating girls here at this school?" John asked.

The room exploded with Lennie's uncontrollable laughter; he lay on the bed holding his sides, pausing only for gasping breaths before roaring again.

"What's so funny?" John asked innocently. "Seems like a normal enough question to me. Men have been looking for women since the garden of Eden. I'll admit this isn't the garden of Eden, but, Lennie, will you stop laughing long enough to tell me what's so funny?"

Lennie made an honest effort to regain his composure. "You haven't heard about President Coote's dating code?"

"No, I haven't. What's so remarkable about it?"

"Sit down, young man. You're in for a rude awakening. Our dating code would stop Samson himself. It goes something like this: the first semester, you can't date—period."

John stared at Lennie in disbelief. "No dates for four and a half months?"

Lennie nodded, still struggling to compose himself. "After that period of celibacy, you may double-date once every two weeks—as long as it's with an IBC student. At the end of the first year, if you're not married out of sheer frustration, you may single-date every other week, but for no more than four and a half hours"—he paused—"provided your school account is paid in full!" Waiting for the full effect to strike his stunned listener, Lennie added with an impish grin, "We have a host of weddings the first week following graduation each year."

Several weeks later, John positively knew that he and the infamous dating code wouldn't coexist peacefully. At first, there was no temptation and no transgression. Then he met Josie Work, a winsome freshman from Bakersfield, a town in his home state of California.

John's personality and magnetic smile had won him the honor of serving as president of his class. Josie was the duly elected secretary-treasurer. Suddenly and mysteriously, there was more "official" work to be done for that class of thirty-seven than for the entire Pentagon. The ever-perceptive eyes of Dean Willard Grimes observed the budding romance with amusement, and the good administrator took steps to close the "official" loopholes. Overnight, John's opportunities to see Josie became more carefully supervised.

The biweekly double-date limitation was too restrictive for this freshman with his strong feelings. One Friday night, John felt that he would absolutely burst if he couldn't see Josie for a few precious minutes. But there was one problem. A religious film was to be shown in the chapel, and attendance was required, unless there was a good reason for being absent. Josie had been excused for a babysitting job, but John couldn't think of any way out. And, most certainly, all seats would be checked by the dean.

Grimes, a World War II veteran and a double amputee, made a special point of checking John's attendance. He was aware that John's dating privileges were exhausted, while his romance was growing. And his seasoned intuition told him John Eils had something up his sleeve.

Standing on tiptoes in his prostheses in the crowded chapel, the dean checked John's chair. He was there—looking dejectedly, but there.

The lights went out, and so did John. He slid to the floor and crawled on all fours up the outside aisle, within inches of the dean. Then he quietly slipped out the double doors and sprinted one mile to the house where Josie was babysitting. Ten minutes of enraptured conversation passed like seconds. After sprinting back to the chapel, John waited until the dean was looking the other way, then dropped to all fours and crawled down the long aisle, delighted that everyone was engrossed in the movie. His timing was perfect. Pulling himself back into his chair, he wiped the perspiration from his brow and ran a comb through his damp hair just as the lights came on. In the same instant, the dean stood to check his seat; to his amazement, John was still there—panting, but there.

SIX

A FOOL FOR CHRIST

One tremendous barrier stood between John and the mission work God had called him to do: his fear of speaking in front of crowds. For John, pulpit ministry was terrifying. He could converse beautifully with one person; but before a group, his tongue grew thick, his face turned crimson, and his knees banged violently against each other.

John knew there was no way he could avoid speaking before large groups. God had talked to him about learning to fly in order to provide masses of unreached people with the gospel. But the very thought of preaching to crowds scared him almost to death.

One spring afternoon, he determined to seek God's help in this matter. After reading every scriptural account he could find of people who had conquered crippling fears, he got down on his knees and asked God to give him total victory over this obstacle.

God answered. That very night, two friends from John's dorm invited him to attend street services and preach with them the next day. The idea of a street service was exciting, but John was paralyzed with fear at the thought of preaching. After thinking it through, however, his versatile imagination conceived a method of ministry that wouldn't require him to open his mouth.

That afternoon, citizens in downtown San Antonio were treated to the sight of a blushing, blond Bible college student strolling up and down the sidewalk of Main Street, wearing a sandwich board constructed of discarded plywood. Those approaching the youthful cleric could easily read the hand-lettered sign: "I'm a fool for Christ."[7] Those words, combined with John's sheepish expression, brought smiles and snickers from passersby. But when they turned around for a second look, many grins faded as they read the other side of the sandwich board: "Whose fool are you?"

After his apprehension had subsided, John began to enjoy carrying that sign and observing people's reactions to it. Gradually, his fear of the public eye disappeared, and he stopped worrying about what people thought of him. For the next three years, he participated in one of the most unique street ministries ever conducted in America.

Its success quickly became the talk of the IBC campus. Joe Bates, the school's skinny, bespectacled bookkeeper, wanted to participate in this dynamic form of street evangelism. He asked John if he might accompany his group the next time they went to minister on the street, and John warmly agreed.

As Saturday approached, Joe noticeably shuffled his feet and shifted his weight in eager anticipation of his great moment in evangelism. At the appropriate time, John turned to him and asked him to step out and say a word for the Lord. Joe sprang into action just as a gang of muscular young men clad in black leather jackets passed by.

"You fellows know you have wages coming to you?" Joe hurled the question at them.

They stopped, turned around, and came back. The largest fellow in the group pressed the issue: "No—what for?"

---

7. This slogan is based on 1 Corinthians 4:10: *"We are fools for Christ's sake, but ye are wise in Christ...."*

"The wages of sin is death!" Joe squeaked nervously.

The gang was not amused. One brawny youth, standing well over six feet and weighing more than two hundred pounds, grabbed the tiny office clerk and lifted him by his coat until his feet dangled like a puppet's. "I'm going to beat you to a pulp," he threatened.

Joe's eyes bulged and rolled toward heaven, and his lips moved silently and swiftly, as if he were uttering a final prayer before martyrdom. After what seemed like an eternity, his assailant—apparently satisfied with the effect he'd had on him—mercifully placed him, unharmed, on terra firma. Joe decided that it might be better if he used a more subtle approach in the future. John readily concurred.

San Antonio had a large Mexican-American population, and John was happy when he discovered that his classmate Mickey Brian could speak fluent Spanish. Another classmate, Earl Naquen, spoke flawless French, and John persuaded his bilingual friends to join him on the downtown streets for a unique experiment: a presentation of the gospel of Jesus Christ in 3-D.

The following Saturday found John Eils on one street corner preaching in English, while Mickey Brian stood on the opposite corner and preached the good news in Spanish. Across the street from Mickey, Earl Naquen shared the gospel in French, which was a mystery to all. Almost no one in San Antonio spoke French, but everyone stopped to listen to this impassioned, finger-pointing foreigner, wondering what he had to say. Regardless, passersby were certain to be caught in the crossfire of Spanish and English issuing from the two opposing street corners.

The major obstacle to this 3-D ministry was traffic noise. One particular Saturday afternoon, the problem was strangely solved, but another scandal was in the making.

A white van came by with two loudspeakers mounted on top, blaring announcements of movies playing at the local theaters.

Not to be outdone, the 3-D gang invaded Main Street the next Saturday with borrowed loudspeakers crowning David Wiggins' 1950 Chevy coupe. For two glorious blocks, the gospel blitzkrieg was a resounding success. Then the flashing red light of a police car terminated their venture. After ordering the team of evangelists to pull over, the annoyed policeman bounded out of his car and walked back to where they were waiting in perplexity and embarrassment.

"Where's your permit for this nonsense?" he demanded.

"We have no permit, officer!" John replied.

"Then follow me, please."

"Where are we going, sir?" John asked courteously.

"To jail," the officer answered.

The vexed officer briskly returned to his squad car, spoke sharply into the two-way radio, and waved for the 3-D gang to follow him. As John pulled out behind the squad car, his thoughts were racing. What a scandal this would be for the school, with some of its best students in jail! And how delighted his father would be if he were dismissed from school! Then the sixty-four-dollar question hit him: Why could the theaters use the public-address system but the 3-D team couldn't?

Ten blocks away from the scene of their arrest, the squad car stopped in front of a white marble building designated by shining metallic letters as the San Antonio Police Department.

The 3-D gospel gang walked in and gave their names and addresses, trying not to appear too shaken. They failed miserably. At the first opportunity, John asked what seemed to be a logical question: "How do you get a permit to have a public-address system on your car?"

"You can't. It's absolutely forbidden!"

"But I saw a truck using a PA system to announce movies last Saturday on the same street!"

"That's different!"

"Not to be disrespectful, sir, but what's the difference?" John pressed the issue.

Realizing that some answer would have to be given to this Bible-carrying nuisance, the officer tried passing the buck. "If you want a permit, go to city hall. They'll tell you the same thing officially." With that, he dismissed the relieved but visibly shaken trio.

At city hall a few days later, they found themselves face-to-face with another official who claimed the theaters could use a PA system but they could not. John sent up a silent prayer as they turned to leave. Suddenly, the official cleared his throat, obviously in preparation for handing down another decision. The trio paused, waiting for his postscript.

"This is off the record"—he halted and pushed his chair back—"but if you should go out there and preach Jesus Christ again over that PA system and get arrested, have the arresting officer call me. I think it will be all right."

And it was. They invaded Houston Street, another of San Antonio's main roads, in English, Spanish, and French, stopping at various places to distribute tracts and talk to interested people. Many conversations ensued.

It was through this ministry that John met Jerry. As he ministered downtown on a Saturday afternoon during his first year at IBC, a tall, slender man approached him, listened to him a moment, and then introduced himself.

"Hello! I'm Dave Witt, a missionary to Durango, Mexico—and this is my son Jerry."

Jerry was lanky and youthful, and John warmed up to him immediately. Upon discovering that Jerry would be spending the weekend in San Antonio, John decided they ought to get together. By the time the weekend was over, John and Jerry's friendship had grown enormously.

"You know what?" John said as they parted ways. "I've got a hunch this won't be the last time we'll be seeing each other."

"I hope not," Jerry said with a grin. "Who knows? Maybe God has something in mind for us."

⟨⟩

John's first year of Bible college was filled with street ministry, hours of study, marvelous chapel services each morning, and Josie. Then summer came, and John returned to Los Angeles to reclaim his position as a seagull supervisor. Little did he know that the Lord had a delightful surprise in store for him.

Walking the sandy beach toward the lifeguard headquarters, he saw a magnificent twenty-foot rescue boat secured to the dock. An unexplainable impulse urged him toward it. Feeling a bit foolish, he climbed up the rope ladder and boarded the beautiful marine craft. It shimmered in the bright sunlight; the wood trim was a rich, dark walnut; the engine purred quietly as the boat was prepared for its daily cruise. As he admired the craftsmanship, the captain approached him.

"May I help you?"

"Yes," John said. "How do you get a job on this boat?"

The captain grinned broadly. "You must have five years of experience as a lifeguard before you can get a job on this boat, and there is a long waiting list."

After thanking the captain for his time, John climbed down the ladder and continued his walk toward lifeguard headquarters. His feelings of foolishness returned. Why had he asked for a job on that particular boat on this particular day? He didn't understand it at the moment, but it was another simple lesson in following the heaven-sent impulse of the Holy Spirit. He learned this the next day, when Jim Barr, captain of the rescue boat, called him at lifeguard headquarters and asked him if he could report to the pier. John enthusiastically replied that he'd be there immediately.

"You want a job as a deck hand on this boat, John?" Captain Barr asked.

"Yes, sir!"

"You're hired. You start this afternoon."

John never did find out what had happened to the waiting list, but he held that job for the next two summers. His most arduous task was polishing the brass and wood immediately after reporting for work at 9:00 a.m. every weekday. After this job was completed, the boat cruised along the Los Angeles beach for an hour and was then anchored for the rest of the day, unless they received an emergency call. John often spent the day with his Bible and banjo, studying and singing. It was the most delightful employment he could imagine. He began sensing God had led him to the boat as part of his preparation for a great work—preparation that was given him one lesson at a time.

The summer passed quickly and pleasantly. On weekends, he worshipped, studied, and visited Josie in Bakersfield whenever he could. At the summer's end, both he and Josie returned to San Antonio and IBC, this time as seasoned students.

SEVEN

"GO ON!
GO ON! GO ON!"

Leonard W. Coote, the founder of IBC, had spent many years as a missionary to Japan. For this reason, the school favored Japan among the countries to which it sent graduates. Thinking that he, too, might become a missionary that nation, John began to study the language under his tutor, IBC President David Coote, Leonard's son. When news came that the elder Coote was returning to the States, John was very excited. He eagerly accepted an invitation to the home of President Coote to meet his father.

The meeting would change the direction of John's life. Knowing in his heart that God had directed him to learn to fly, he shared his concept of evangelism by airplane with Leonard Coote. The response he received was completely negative. "No planes are needed in Japan!" Leonard Coote's words were blunt, and for John, they ruled out the idea of going to Japan to do missionary work.

The question, now bigger than life itself, loomed before him: Where did God want him to go? God answered that question in less than a week. Wilbur Hunt, maintenance supervisor at IBC, invited John to go with him to Monterrey, Mexico, to visit the headquarters of the mission work of Harold Brian. John eagerly accepted the invitation, not knowing that the trip was one of divine destiny.

They made the 300-mile trip in a Dodge pickup. It was John's first visit to Mexico, and he was fascinated by his surroundings. Upon arriving at their destination, they were greeted warmly by Harold Brian, and immediate plans were made for a trip the next day to Laguna Sanchez—a mission across the mountain—where they would hold a service. The following day at noon, the Dodge pickup was loaded with nine American students and missionaries, in addition to as many Mexicans as the truckbed could hold. Long after the vehicle was loaded to capacity, would-be passengers were still trying to get in. Realizing the danger of an overloaded truck, Brian ordered, "No one else get in! There's no more room." The statement was received with obvious disappointment by those who were turned away. John was astounded at their eagerness to ride several hours in the back of a pickup truck just to attend a church service. What was their motivation, he wondered—the church service or the ride? Probably the latter.

One Mexican shouted something in Spanish as they began the journey to Laguna Sanchez.

"What did he say?" John asked.

"He said they would see us tomorrow in Laguna Sanchez."

"And where's that?"

"It's sixty-five kilometers away—over the mountain."

John laughed. "He's just trying to make us feel good. They can't possibly get there!"

⌒

The one-truck gospel army arrived at Laguna Sanchez at nine o'clock that evening. Church was announced with a simple toot of the truck horn. People came scrambling from all directions.

The church at Laguna Sanchez was a one-room structure measuring thirty feet by fifteen feet. It was supported by stucco walls, and the thatched roof was made of palm leaves. The natives had made the walls by weaving branches between large tree trunks and then pressing mud into the lacework. In the United States, a room of this size would seat no more than fifty people; but there were more than 400 people crowded into the church that night.

After Harold Brian had preached a very long sermon (by US standards), every one of the visiting Americans gave his or her testimony in detail and at length. As they spoke, the copper-colored Mexican faces reflected rapt attention. Those people were so eager, so open, so spiritually starved, that John's heart began to ache. When the spiritual extravaganza ended, a little after midnight, he knew the villagers must be weary beyond the point of exhaustion. American churchgoers would have walked out long before now.

What happened next was beyond John's wildest imagination. The *alcalde*—the elected village leader, or mayor—approached Brian, and it was obvious to all that he was making an earnest appeal. Although John didn't understand what the man was saying, he could see disappointment written all over his broad face. As Brian shook his head no, John stepped up and asked, "Harold, what does he want?"

Brian replied, "He wants the church service to continue."

"Continue?" John murmured in utter disbelief. "But it's way past midnight!"

"He knows that better than you; he'll have to work all day tomorrow. These people are poor farmers who work like slaves in the fields just to stay alive."

John was absolutely stunned. If the people wanted them to continue the service, why shouldn't they? "I'm for staying as long as they want to stay," John volunteered. "That is, if it's all right with you, Harold."

Harold agreed, and the village leader asked everyone to preach at least one more time. So the round began again, with Harold interpreting. It was well after three in the morning when the service finally ended. Even at that hour, several people urged them to "Go on! Go on! Go on!" Some members of the congregation slept all night on the dirt floor of the church, to ensure they would have a seat for the service the following afternoon.

As John lay down on one of the crude benches, he gave awe-filled thanks to God for the hunger of these simple people for the good news of Jesus Christ. But he was yet to learn how deep and impelling that hunger really was.

⌒

The next morning, John had an experience that sealed his calling to Mexico. It had been a short night. The bench he'd slept on wasn't the softest bed he'd ever used, and his back ached. He stood up wearily, yawned, and walked outside to get a drink. It was then that he saw a group of fifty Mexicans—men, women, and children—whom they had left behind in Monterrey the day before. They had walked through the mountains all day and all night to attend the church service this morning. As John saw them cresting the hill, he felt a lump forming in his throat, and tears brimmed in his eyes.

"Oh, God, forgive me!" John whimpered under his breath. "Where have I been so long? I never knew how much they wanted You!"

He was embarrassed at his own lack of spiritual fervor, and he grieved at the thought of so many American Christians who find it difficult to get to church even in their high-powered automobiles.

A spontaneous prayer came from his lips: "Lord, help me reach these people! They're so desperate, so needy, and so abandoned!"

John knew he had found his people—he was home. Mexico was to be his place of ministry, his valley of tears, his mountain peak of triumph. John Eils had received his calling and commission from almighty God.

EIGHT

MARRIAGE AND MIRACLES

John's last two years at IBC passed quickly, even though Josie was not on campus his senior year. She had dropped out of school to support a broken family. On June 27, 1958, four weeks after John's graduation, he and Josie married at her home church in Bakersfield, California.

At the ceremony, John was nervous beyond description. His was the first wedding he had ever attended, and because of an unexpected funeral at the church the day before, there had been no time to rehearse. Sensing the bridegroom's nervousness, Pastor Paul Winter was deliberately slow in leading them through the marriage vows. Even so, John stumbled over the words as though trying to speak in a foreign language. When instructed to put the ring on Josie's finger, he offered his hand to her.

Finally, it was over, and the amused minister officially pronounced John and Josie as husband and wife. The flustered bridegroom stood at attention, waiting for the next step. There was none. It was a very long moment before he heard Josie instructing him to lift her veil, kiss her, and then escort her down the aisle toward the front door. He dutifully obeyed, and they were officially wed—thanks to God.

Honeymoons cost money; therefore, the newlyweds didn't take one. Neither of them really cared. There would never have to be another cloak-and-dagger meeting to evade the omniscient eyes of Dean Grimes. They were together at last.

At first, they lived with Josie's parents, but they hoped that situation wouldn't last long. Josie was just as eager to get off to Mexico as John was. He had told her all about the spiritual hunger of the people there, and the more she thought about it, the more restless she became to go. Though she had natural desires for a home and children, she knew she could never be satisfied with being an average American housewife.

⌒

Many young couples who have made a commitment to mission work fall into the trap of materialism. They buy a new car and rent a house "just for a few months." They purchased a stove, refrigerator, dishes, furniture, and maybe even a television set. Soon, they are deeply in debt, and one or both of them must find work to pay the bills.

Sometimes, before they are debt free, a baby appears, or the car needs major repair. Weeks turn into months, and months turn into years, and they are still far from the mission field to which God had called them.

John and Josie easily could have fallen into this trap. Both had come from broken homes, and this was their first opportunity to achieve security. John had been tempted many times to postpone his entrance into the mission field, but each time, he'd been reminded of fifty Mexicans walking over the rugged mountains for more than twelve brutal hours to attend one church service. Every day he delayed was a day the people he had come to love would have to do without something they cherished—the gospel.

In John's three years at IBC, God had taught him that He was able to give absolute direction for every occasion and every material need the occasion entailed. God had directed John and Josie to Mexico, and their only immediate need was for transportation to get there.

In John's shirt pocket was a letter he had received a few days earlier from Dave Witt, the missionary in Durango, Mexico. It was an invitation to come work with him, on the condition that they raise their own support. Friends had given them exactly two hundred dollars, and they somehow had to buy a car with that amount. That would leave them no money for gas, but they were depending on God to supply their needs one at a time, and always on time.

With no knowledge of their financial situation, Josie's brother-in-law phoned John a few days later. "Hey! I found a 1950 white V-8 Ford for two hundred dollars. Are you interested?"

"Does it run?" John asked, laughing.

"The man says it's in great shape!"

"I'll be over to look at it. Where are you?"

After getting directions, John hung up the phone and charged out the door.

The car had 150,000 miles on it, and the oil gauge didn't work. Nevertheless, it was a form of transportation, and it was within their means. John paid the seller and proudly drove the car home to his new bride.

Now that transportation was available, there was no need to delay their departure for Mexico any longer. That very day, they packed everything they owned into the backseat of the car and kissed their weeping parents good-bye.

Paul Winter walked with them to the dilapidated car. He was moved by their great commitment. "I want to give you this money to help you get started," he told them. "It's not much, but God wants you to have it." The pastor reached inside the car and dropped twenty-five dollars into Josie's lap. God had provided the money to buy gas!

John thanked the minister warmly, then started the "bargain car" and aimed it toward El Paso, Texas. As they rattled off, Josie waved a final time to the group of weeping parents huddled there, her own vision blurred by tears. The adventure of faith had begun!

John had charted a course that would carry them through El Centro, California, to Phoenix, Arizona, and finally to El Paso, Texas, where they would then cross the border into Juárez, Mexico. The car performed beautifully—for the first fifty miles. Then they noticed that the humming sound coming from the right rear wheel had grown steadily louder into a whine. John watched anxiously as the miles registered on the odometer, as if his constant vigil would make the car perform properly.

A few miles from El Centro, John glanced in the rearview mirror and saw smoke. After pulling over and examining the right rear wheel, he realized the smoke had been coming from the bearing. The wheel was so hot, he burned his hand when he touched the hub.

Trying to hide his anxiety from Josie, John climbed back into the car and said something about having the wheel checked in El Centro. Neither of them mentioned the gnawing question on their minds: Where would they get the money for repairs? They had just enough money for gas to reach El Paso.

By the time they reached El Centro, the whining had escalated to a scream, and the smoke looked like the exhaust from a locomotive. Pulling into the first service station he saw, John was greeted by a jovial attendant who announced, "Hey, your right rear wheel bearing is burned out!" The attendant's voice had a mirthful ring that John had a hard time responding to.

"What will it cost to be fixed?" he managed.

"Oh, about nine dollars fifty-eight cents for labor and parts." His flying pencil confirmed his estimate as he wrote the sum in bold numbers at the bottom of a work order. "Shall we fix it?"

"There is no way I can afford it, friend. We'll have to come up with something else," John replied dejectedly.

"You'd better try a miracle, pal. This car has had it!"

John got back in the car, started the engine, and bravely drove out of the station. Spotting a roadside park on the next block, he pulled in and parked the screaming, smoking vehicle. It sounded like a Sherman tank and looked like a rolling fireball. Josie's face mirrored John's dejection.

"Josie," John began, with a strange determination in his tone, "I feel we should make a covenant with each other right here."

"About what?" Josie was curious.

"About things like this. I think we should agree right here that, wherever this venture of faith takes us, we will never make begging appeals for money. Whenever we have a need, whatever it is, no matter how large or small, we will ask God to provide for us. The first day He quits providing, we'll quit, too!"

"That's fine, John. Now, what do we do about this car?"

Josie's question was very practical. What would he do? They were still hundreds of miles from their destination, but their car seemed to have reached its end already.

The words of the station attendant flashed through John's mind: "Try a miracle, pal." That was the answer—a miracle!

"Josie, get out of the car!" John exclaimed. "We're going to pray for this rattle trap!"

She got out and obediently stood beside her husband. What a strange thing to pray for—a wheel bearing! John began, "Lord, if You had the power to open blind eyes, heal deaf ears, and cause a dead man to come back to life, there is hope for this Ford. If You want us to get to Mexico, please take care of this wheel bearing. In Jesus' name, amen."

They got back in the car, started the engine, and eased into the fast-moving California traffic. Both were totally silent, listening intently. They heard no noise as they pulled away from the park; none as they gathered speed. Finally, they were traveling sixty miles per hour, and there wasn't a hum to be heard. No screaming steel, no smoke, no trouble!

"He did it! He did it! God fixed that wheel bearing!" they both shouted at once. The wheel bearing had been repaired by the Master Mechanic and was functioning perfectly. God had provided again!

They drove a few more miles as night began to settle on the California desert. Pulling into another roadside park, John said, "I'm so excited, I doubt if I'll be able to sleep—but let's try."

⌒

A brilliant orange sun rose over the California desert the next morning, waking the sleeping travelers. They folded back their blanket, had a brief time of devotions, and then directed the car into the blazing desert. Today's trip to El Paso would be a hot one.

Both were elated over yesterday's maintenance miracle, which had been confirmed that morning by the total absence of smoke and noise. But by ten o'clock, both knew they were in trouble again; the radiator was boiling over. Yesterday, smoke had been pouring from the rear; today, the front end was steaming.

The car boiled over sixteen times before they reached El Paso. John had poured enough water into the radiator to put out the

Great Chicago Fire. He consoled Josie by telling her they would get all the "bugs" out of the car before they got to Mexico. In his heart, however, he knew the only way to exterminate all the bugs from this junk heap would be to incinerate it.

The Eilses steam engine chugged into the city limits of El Paso late that evening. They had been invited to spend the night with Pastor A. O. Moore, who had been an instructor at IBC before coming to a church in El Paso.

The next morning, Pastor Moore invited John to speak to his congregation of fifty parishioners about his plans for Mexico. John and Josie were true to their covenant: they did not tell anyone about the radiator.

After the service, a man came straight up to John and began speaking rather apologetically. "I hope you don't think I'm out of my mind, but the Lord impressed upon me while you were speaking to ask you about the radiator on your car!"

John grinned broadly. "No, I don't think you're out of your mind at all. My radiator boiled over sixteen times yesterday. Something's probably wrong with it!" He was laughing out loud at this point.

"Yes, I'd say so!" agreed the parishioner. "I have a radiator shop near here. If you'll bring your car down in the morning, I'll fix it like new—with no charge!" He shoved his business card into John's hand and left.

God had provided again! It was thrilling—it was unbelievable—and it was only the beginning! The more John and Josie counted the blessings they had, the less they craved the luxuries they went without.

NINE

MEXICO AND MADNESS

The next afternoon, John and Josie invaded Mexico via Juárez. The radiator had been fixed, and Pastor Moore had given them twenty-five dollars, which was all they had.

After inspecting their luggage and the car's interior, the customs officer placed a six-month tourist sticker on their windshield and motioned them toward the vast interior of Mexico.

They felt like they were entering a new world as they drove through the narrow streets of Juárez. The air was filled with strange sounds of Spanish and with strong odors that suggested sanitary services were few.

Raw meat covered with flies hung in the open market. The streets were filled with donkey-drawn carts, which added to the scent and scenery. Many donkeys wore bright-colored sombreros on their heads, their ears poking through specially cut holes. Other cart merchants decorated their animals with bright flowers attached to their ears or laced to their lower harnesses.

The buildings were a mixture of madness and mansions. There are two classes of people in Mexico: the very rich and the unbelievably poor. Since there are no zoning laws, it is not uncommon to see an elaborate mansion surrounded by adobe slums. To keep out the tidal wave of poverty and filth, the mansions are often surrounded by high stone walls topped with iron spikes.

John's heart ached for the poor of this country. They were the people to whom he would minister. The awesome realization that this land of charm and chaos would be his home, and these people his parishioners, slowly dawned on him.

"Look for road signs, Josie!" he said, "We'll head in the general direction of Durango!"

He didn't know how true that statement was. They drove more than two hundred miles "in the general direction of Durango" before they saw a sign confirming that they were, indeed, going in the right direction.

They saw many varieties of traffic. Sometimes they were almost blown off the road by buses going eighty miles per hour; at other times, their chug-along Ford managed to pass a donkey-drawn cart. A few times, they were compelled to stop altogether for a cow lazily crossing the road. They went over many bridges wide enough for only one car. If two cars happened to approach the bridge at the same time, the driver who honked his horn louder got to go first.

The Ford functioned well throughout the day, considering all it had been through. When night fell, it seemed blacker than any darkness John or Josie had ever experienced before. There were no roadside parks, lighted highways, or blinking neon signs—just absolute blackness.

They drove into the town of Camargo and selected a choice spot for the night in their favorite motel—the Ford. Josie had a few questions to ask before they went to sleep.

"How are we going to locate Dave Witt tomorrow when we get to Durango?"

"The letter says that everyone there knows him as the 'tall American,' so all we have to do is ask around," John replied. He expected Durango to be a small village, where a tall American would stand above the crowd.

They slept, but not very soundly. Both were glad when the sun rose. The journey continued with mounting excitement as time zipped past, bringing them closer to the "village" of Durango.

When they topped the mountain range and saw the sprawling metropolis before them, their mouths dropped open. Josie gave expression to John's thoughts: "How are we ever going to find Dave Witt in this big city?"

"Where did we ever get the idea this was a small village?" John asked, equally incredulous.

Both were silent as their car slipped into the city and was swallowed by people, shops, buildings, and businesses. John found a place to park and set out on foot to look for a "tall American." If he could just speak a little Spanish! The citizens of Durango took great interest in this blond gringo walking the streets, looking at the face of each tall man he passed. Many people tried helping him, but the language barrier proved insurmountable. John had never felt more awkward in his life.

He spotted an ambulance parked at the curb. The driver stood on the sidewalk, talking to a pretty Mexican girl. Thinking the driver might be bilingual, John asked him for assistance. No luck! As he started walking again, he heard a moan coming from the interior of the battered ambulance. Looking inside, he saw someone lying on a stretcher, presumably waiting to be taken to the hospital. It would seem the poor patient would have to wait until the lovesick driver was done cooing over his sweetheart. John shook his head and walked on.

He searched until dark, while Josie waited patiently in the car. Dave Witt was nowhere to be found. John returned to the car and recounted about his futile search to Josie as they drove around looking for a place to spend the night. They found an inexpensive motel and paid for the room in advance.

Once inside their room, they checked how much money they had and found themselves in possession of ninety-six cents. Food in Mexico was even more expensive than in the States. There would be no restaurant meal tonight. As they looked at the small amount of change on the bed between them, a feeling of loneliness overwhelmed them. The streets were filled with people they couldn't talk to; the newspapers were full of print they couldn't read; their radio was a plastic parrot spouting phrases in an unknown tongue; and the one person they knew in that city of ninety thousand souls couldn't be found! They felt completely lost.

Realizing that their feeling of desolation was partly due to hunger, Josie went out to the car and found a pint of canned apples her mother had sent along "just in case," while John bought some crackers with the money they had left. After eating a meager supper in their room, they realized they had nothing for tomorrow—but then, tomorrow wasn't here yet.

The next morning, John awoke with a brilliant thought. Every missionary has to go to the mailbox sooner or later. He dressed quickly, as did Josie. She wasn't about to wait behind again.

Locating the post office, they wrote a note and attached it to Dave Witt's box, then went outside and sat on the steps to wait. Within three hours, they were "discovered" by the "tall American."

"Dave," John said, "right now, I don't know of anybody who looks any better to me than you do!" He paused, before adding with a sheepish grin, "Unless it might be Josie!"

TEN

THE GREAT SHOOTING CONTEST

A week after the Eils' arrival in Durango, Dave Witt left for the states to visit supporting churches there. John and Josie weren't left alone in the Witt home, though; they had the company of Dave's son, Jerry, who was only three years younger than John.

Mexico was a new world! The rules of society were drastically different. People walked slowly, talked slowly, and slept in the middle of the day. Businesses, without exception, shut down for an hour every day at noon for a siesta. Bribery was a way of life. If you went to jail guilty but with money, the latter would save you. If you went to jail innocent but poor—God help you! Nightlife revolved around a central plaza where young and old gathered to read newspapers and listen to broadcasts on transistor radios. Once a week, a state-supported band played in the plaza, while the citizens sat on wooden benches and listened to the music until ten o'clock in the evening.

One of the very first lessons these youthful missionaries learned was a thing called "Montezuma's revenge," known in America as "diarrhea." Ten days after a bout, and ten pounds lighter, two wiser, thinner missionaries had learned to watch everything they ate. There are some things gringos simply should not eat in Mexico. It was like boot camp: rigorous mental and physical preparation for the unknown. John and Josie abandoned the old cliché "What you don't know won't hurt you." What you don't know in Mexico may well kill you!

Caution was becoming a way of life. Each morning before breakfast, John took a quick walk down to the plaza and back. On one of his first morning walks, he was horrified when a house-wife came to her front door with a bucket of yellow liquid and carelessly threw it into the street. His imagination gave it a name. As he continued his walk, he found yellow puddles everywhere, up and down the sidewalks. Returning home, he shared about the horrible lack of sanitation he'd come across.

Jerry roared with laughter. "That's not what you think! These people make tortillas out of corn. They soak the tough corn in water with lime to break down the outer hull."

"The corn— Oh, I see!" John felt a bit foolish.

After his morning walk to the plaza, John would return home to eat whatever was available for breakfast. Then he'd go to his Spanish class, which lasted well into the night. The first month, John and Josie received sixty-five dollars from friends in America. After paying their Spanish instructor, filling their gas tank, and buying a few necessary items, they had enough money left to pur-chase all the pancake mix they needed to keep them alive. So, they ate pancakes three times a day.

For entertainment, they went to the airport. Jerry's descrip-tion of the events that occurred at the Mexican airport had been so hilarious that John had decided to go and see for himself. He'd found it all true.

It was common for Tigres Voladores, a Mexican commercial airline, to start the engines of its DC-3 planes using a long rope pulled by twenty-five to thirty Mexicans. John watched as the rope was looped over the prop and the "mechanics" were lined up, ready to pull. At the command *"Jale!"*[8] they strained the rope, and the huge engine backfired. In an instant, thirty Mexicans were thrown all over the pavement as the prop reversed itself. It took more than a little effort for the "chief mechanic" to persuade his skinned-up troops to get in line again for another kamikaze attempt at starting the engine.

The next try proved successful, and the second engine started from the power created by the first. When both engines were ready, John prepared to watch the takeoff. But it was a long time coming!

On the first run down the airstrip, the pilot directed the plane near all the holes in the pavement so the wind from the propellers would blow the water out of them. With the airstrip dry, a second run was made to determine whether the plane would clear the barbed-wire fence at the end of the runway. It didn't look as though it would, so the pilot took immediate steps to decelerate the aircraft as quickly as possible. Then he turned around and came back to the terminal. After several barrels of gasoline had been removed, he made a third attempt down the airstrip, and this time, takeoff was achieved. John concluded that people who travel by plane in Mexico certainly get their money's worth!

⌒

Returning from the municipal airport one afternoon, John and Jerry decided to stop at Bill Brown's Flying Service. Bill was an expert pilot who chartered flights by single-engine plane all over Mexico. As they got out of the car, Bill approached them.

"You guys are just the people I wanted to talk to!"

Jerry laughed. "What did we do now?"

"Nothing! I was just wondering if you'd be interested in making two hundred dollars."

---

8. *"Jale!"*: "Pull!"

"Sure!" John replied without thinking. "What do we have to do?"

"One of my planes crashed, and I want you to get it out of the mountains. You can transport it by hitching my four-wheel trailer behind your Ford."

"We'll do it—right now!" John hesitated a moment, then added, "When do we get paid?"

"As soon as you pull the plane onto this property!"

"One plane coming up!" John answered.

They picked up the trailer and headed out of Durango toward the mountains. Jerry drove, while John checked the map to determine the approximate position of the plane. He had a strange feeling that they were in for more than they had bargained for.

Less than an hour's drive down the highway, Jerry glanced out the window. "Hey, John, our trailer is passing us!" he almost screamed.

John laughed in disbelief as the trailer shot past them. Jerry began braking. The trailer plowed into a deep ditch beside the highway, careened right back onto the pavement, and flipped over several times before stopping upside down in the middle of the highway.

Jerry stopped the car, and he and John stared at the wreckage in shock. After crawling out of the Ford, they tried desperately to get the trailer on its wheels. But it wouldn't budge—not even slightly.

"You know, friend," Jerry commented, "we just might be in for some serious trouble."

"What do you mean?" John replied, furrowing his brow.

"It just occurred to me that two things are wrong, John. One: You are a tourist in Mexico and can't work for wages. Second: We're going to need help getting this trailer right-side up, and that means the rurales will probably be the ones to help us. If they find out you're getting paid for this job, we're sunk."

"Who are the rurales?" This was another thing John didn't know about Mexico.

"They're the rural police officers of Mexico, and they're tough—very, very tough. If a crime is committed in their area, and several days pass without it being solved, they blame it on the next person who breaks a law of any kind."

While Jerry was talking, John could see a tandem truck barreling down the road toward them. Jerry saw it, too, and knew it was too late to do anything. It was the rurales. Jerry had lived in Mexico for years and knew the Mexican people well. His brain raced for a way to get them out of this ridiculous mess.

The truck stopped, and a group of soldiers got out. Jerry gave John one last-minute order: "Let me do all the talking; you just play along with anything I come up with."

"What are you going to do?" John quizzed.

"I don't know yet, but you'd better pray I think of something soon. We'll be in jail tonight if I don't."

A man who appeared to be a major approached with the distinct swagger common among rurales. "What goes on here? Whose trailer is this? Where's your license? Where's your permit for the trailer?"

The questions came like bullets from a machine gun. And they had no chance to answer any of them. Jerry started to reply when the major's attention was drawn to the .22 rifle in the rear seat of the Ford.

"Whose rifle is this?" he demanded. Without allowing anyone to answer, he announced to his troops that he was the best shot in all of Mexico.

In an instant, Jerry had his answer. It just might work...

"Well, that's very interesting," Jerry began in Spanish. "You're the finest shot in all of Mexico, and my friend here, Señor John, is the champion rifleman in the whole state of Texas!" Jerry paused for a moment. "Why don't we have a shooting contest? If you beat my friend, you'll be the greatest rifleman in all of Mexico *and* Texas—and Texas has the greatest rifle shooters in the world!"

It was working. The green-clad rurales were gathering around, eagerly awaiting the major's response to this challenge. Jerry knew that the major could not afford to lose face before his troops. A long moment passed, however, before he accepted.

John was standing by, completely ignorant of the scheme his fast-thinking friend had devised. The whole conversation had taken place in very rapid Spanish, which he didn't understand very well.

"You're in a rifle shooting contest with the major," Jerry explained to him. He claims to be the best in Mexico. I told him you were the best in Texas. I know these people, John, and I have one word of advice for you: when we set up the targets, whatever you do, miss."

As they talked, two rurales walked into the field with several Coke bottles. The major was carefully inspecting his rifle to insure the certainty of his victory in this momentous shootout. Jerry gave John a pat on the back and further urged him, "Lose, baby—lose badly!"

The major was up first. He took aim at the glittering Coke bottle, which had been set up approximately one hundred fifty feet away. He fired and missed.

John gave them a real show. Moistening the bead on the rifle so that it would shine in the sunlight, he took great pains to wrap his arm in a leather sling just as he swung the gun smoothly to his shoulder. He fired and missed. The rurales cheered in total delight. Their leader was still in contention.

The bottles were brought closer, at a distance of about a one hundred feet. John began laughing. He leaned toward Jerry and whispered, "I can hit that with a rock!"

"Get serious, John, it's jail if you win!"

There was another volley. The major hit his bottle, and so did John. Jerry was far from happy, but John laughed at the look on his panic-stricken face.

On the third attempt, the major connected, but John missed. The rurales shouted in triumph; Jerry smiled in relief. Walking up to the major, Jerry put his arm around the man's shoulders and announced to the captive audience, "This is the greatest shot in all of Mexico and Texas—and probably the world!"

The major seemed very impressed. In a show of modesty, he admitted that what Jerry had said was, without doubt, the living truth.

After congratulating the major repeatedly, Jerry asked him a very pointed question: "What should we do about our trailer?"

"Oh, yes. Well, I see no problem here," the major announced officiously. He gave a few piercing orders, and the troopers scrambled to get the trailer right-side up. Observing the broken tongue, the major then ordered the troops to take the trailer to the next town to have it welded. Then he turned to John and Jerry and said, "Let's go!"

"Where are we going?" Jerry replied, fighting inner fear. Had the whole scheme failed after all?

"To lunch, amigo, to lunch!" the major said in a slow Spanish drawl. When they arrived at the restaurant he selected, he announced to everyone that he had just beaten the champion rifleman in Texas.

The major paid for the meal, then took the two John and Jerry back to their car, to which the troopers had already attached the repaired trailer. After offering their congratulations to the major again, John and Jerry drove off, with the troops smiling and waving behind them.

"That was pretty tricky," John teased when they were en route to retrieve the plane. "I never realized what a mess I was getting us into."

Jerry just grinned and said nothing. Later that night, they both had to have a little "talk with the Lord" about their tricky tactics.

The money John received for the job was a great help, as it allowed him and Josie to catch up on some household expenses, but there still wasn't enough for the much-desired flying lessons. He and Josie made it a matter of united prayer. Flying was not to be a hobby for him; it was to be his means of reaching remote villages to spread the gospel. John looked into flying lessons and learned that they would cost exactly eighty dollars.

Several weeks passed, and nothing happened. As the pressure of other costs mounted, John wondered if he would know how to spend the money that came in—whether to put it toward flying lessons or use it for other needs. He told God he would wait to receive a check for exactly eighty dollars, to ensure it was God's provision for flying lessons. Within a matter of days, a letter came from Kansas City containing a check for exactly eighty dollars. John began his flying lessons that afternoon.

His instructor did not speak English, and John was still struggling with his Spanish. The learning experience became a "monkey see, monkey do" process. John would watch his instructor and then imitate him. If he performed correctly, the instructor would give him two pats on the back. If he made a mistake, the instructor would shake his head emphatically.

As the days turned into weeks, John's Spanish became more and more fluent and his flying technique exceptional. All the while, he and Josie were gaining valuable knowledge about the mad and marvelous country of Mexico. After John earned his pilot's license, they felt sure that their toughest times were over.

In fact, they were on a mountain peak, and the valley that lay before them would be the darkest they had ever experienced.

ELEVEN

A NIGHT WITHOUT STARS

A few days after he obtained his pilot's license, John came across an ad in the morning newspaper that sent his spirits soaring: *American aircraft, Aeronca Champion. Mexican registration. Needs repair. 1250 pesos.*

A Monterrey address was listed. Since the location was within driving distance, John returned home and persuaded Jerry Witt to drive with him to Monterrey to look at the plane.

The two of them decided it would be wise to bring along Sam McKenzie, a missionary friend from Durango who knew a great deal about planes. Sam was also a pilot, and he shared John's dream of an "airplane ministry"; and the two of them had talked and prayed a lot about future opportunities. It comforted John to know two men who not only knew planes but also understood his desire to reach Mexico's poor with the gospel.

When they reached at the small dirt airstrip on the outskirts of Monterrey, the occupants of the still-functioning Ford scrambled out. The airport manager graciously intercepted them as they walked toward the hangars. "Buenos dias, amigos!"

"Buenos dias!" John held up the newspaper. "We would like to see the plane advertised for sale."

Recognizing the ad, the manager led them toward a closed hangar.

"This airplane needs a lot of work." His extended arms and arched eyebrows dramatized the point. When he opened the door to the hangar, John was an instant believer.

The Aeronca Champion looked like a featherless fowl. There was no fabric anywhere on the craft anywhere, no engine, no instruments—just a bare metal frame with wheels. Not exactly a luxury aircraft, but the price reflected its condition.

Noticing John's fallen countenance, Sam said, "Don't worry, John. This plane can be fixed. It'll take work. The fabric for the shell, an engine, and the necessary instruments should run about fifteen hundred dollars."

"And where will we get fifteen hundred dollars?" John asked.

"Maybe you'll have to go to the States and raise it from churches willing to support you," Sam suggested.

"But do you think we can make this plane tough enough to land in and take off from pastures in small villages?" John was trying to settle some of his doubts.

"I think so," Sam replied optimistically.

John and Jerry walked around the plane, shaking the wings and checking the strength of the metal frame, in an effort to expose any structural flaw.

Satisfied at last, John removed the "For Sale" sign. "I'll take it!"

"Bueno—bueno, amigo!" said the airport manager. "But you will have to drive into town to transfer the title to your name."

"All right—we'll do that today and wrap the whole thing up. Will it be possible for me to leave the plane here until I go to the States to raise the funds to repair it?"

"Si!" The manager then explained the rental policy at the hangar. The plane could stay there indefinitely.

After the arrangements were complete, the three men returned to the car and drove several miles before Sam broke the silence.

"John, have you ever heard of the Wings of a Dove organization in California?"

"No, what is it?" John queried.

"It's an organization of businessmen who are interested in spreading the good news in Mexico through gospel tracts dropped from low-flying aircraft."

"Sounds exciting! That's exactly what I plan to do when we get the plane repaired."

After a momentary pause, Sam continued. "They want me to be their number one pilot in Mexico. What do you think about working with me and this organization?"

The very thought was thrilling. John's response was explosive and ecstatic. "Beautiful! Beautiful! It just sounds too good to be true, Sam!"

"We'll soon know for sure," Sam continued. "The organization has asked me to come to their convention in California next week to discuss the details of such a ministry. How about going with me?" Without waiting for the obvious answer, Sam told him, "I'd like you to be my top assistant. We'll work together all the way and be in full-time ministry with the airplane."

John was in orbit. This was exactly what he wanted to do. It was working out so well that God must have been behind it!

The next morning, John and Josie began packing for California. At last, they had arrived as missionaries! They would go to the States, raise money for the plane repairs, attend the convention with Sam, and return to Durango for a heart-stirring missionary ministry.

On the first day of the convention, John and Sam attended the morning service together. Then the officers who determined organizational policy met behind closed doors. Within minutes, they sent for Sam. John waited patiently in the hall for what seemed like an eternity.

When Sam came out of the closed session thirty minutes later, John could tell something was wrong. "They want to see you, John." Sam's voice was void of emotion.

John followed Sam into a room where a dozen men sat around one large table. He felt a little nervous. It looked like they were the jury, and he the case in question.

Sam introduced John to the officers, who acknowledged the introduction politely but a bit stiffly. John was invited to sit. Then followed a long silence, which was broken at last by a man to John's left.

"Mr. Eils, what are your plans for Mexico?"

"Well, I plan to work with Sam as his top assistant." John began. "We have discussed distributing gospel tracts by plane and have agreed that we would like to work as a team."

"How many flying hours do you have?"

"I just received my license," John replied. He realized he was very green, but that would wear off with experience.

Again, there was silence and an exchange of glances around the table. Then the presiding chairman made the most shattering statement John had ever heard in his adult life.

"The truth is, Mr. Eils, you are absolutely useless to us. You don't have enough flying time, you have little missionary ability, and you are not yet fluent in the language."

John was speechless. This was surely a bad dream.

The chairman continued, "I'm afraid, Mr. Eils, you would be a detriment to our organization, not an asset. The blunt truth is, we have no room for you!"

John felt stripped to the bone, as if he had plunged into a tank of savage piranhas. He looked despairingly at Sam for help.

"I'm sorry, John; that's the way it is," Sam said. "I'm working with these fellows now. You'll have to work on your own."

John fought back the hot tears welling in his eyes and tried to swallow the lump in his throat. Forcing his rubbery legs to move, he pushed his chair back and made his way to the door.

Walking down the endless hall, he felt numb with despair. What would he tell Josie? His family and friends?

He returned to the motel and poured out his heart to Josie, who received the news with silent sorrow. Finally, he verbalized the question that had haunted him since the meeting: "Where do we go from here, Josie?"

"Well," Josie said, "there'll be a missionary convention at IBC soon. Why don't we go there?"

It was a long, silent trip to San Antonio. By the time John and Josie reached their destination, John had resolved to turn to the man who had been both friend and father to him while he was in college—David Coote.

In San Antonio, John drove straight to IBC, arriving a week before the convention began. The bleak campus and humble buildings now looked like the suburbs of heaven. President Coote seemed delighted to see him and listened sympathetically to his bad news.

"John," Coote began, "why don't you work here at the college with the maintenance department until you get your bearings again? God has His hand on you, and I assure you that you're not useless. Every ministry has mountain peaks of triumph and dark valleys of despair."

He paused, looking as though he was collecting his thoughts, then continued, "Moses murdered an Egyptian and spent forty years in the desert getting the patience that qualified him to do what he, as an eighty-year-old sheepherder, could not do as the son of Pharaoh.

"No, you are not useless. God uses simple instruments for mighty victories. David used a sling to slay Goliath, while Saul's sword and armor were useless. Moses led six million people with a mere stick, but God was in it. Christ won the great victory for us on a crude Roman cross. Little is much, John, when God is in it!

"It's dark now—very dark—it always is just before the dawn. God is not looking for men impressed with their own ability and aptitude. He looks for men who are simply available. That's you!"

David Coote was tall, thin, and powerfully persuasive. His words were like healing oil on John's wound. Arching his bushy eyebrows in his usual manner of dramatic expression, he continued, "Josie can work in the kitchen and boost your income. You won't get rich, but you won't starve, either. You can stay in the duplex apartment until things work out."

John expressed his deep gratitude as best as he could. President Coote's kind offer was like a life preserver held out to a drowning man. He and Josie now had a place to sleep, food to eat, and jobs to work.

Still, there were times when John felt like a complete failure and misfit. The thought of the approaching missionary convention was depressing. He wanted to go, but he dreaded having to face his classmates—many of whom were already serving in foreign countries. He knew he had no answer for the question he would be asked many times: "How are you doing?"

John purposely arrived late for the first service of the convention and chose a seat in the rear of the church, so that He could slip out undetected and unquestioned when the service was over.

From the time the service began, the presence of the Holy Spirit was obvious. The singing rang through Revival Temple in San Antonio with spontaneous unity and anointing. Congregational prayer time was generously sprinkled with the sweet and sacred prayer language of the Spirit-filled.

The guest speaker was missionary-evangelist Dave Shock. Immediately after he was introduced, he left the platform and, to everyone's amazement, walked down the center aisle of the church. Where was he going? The evangelist walked straight toward John, whom he didn't even know. He placed his hands on John's head, and his booming voice filled the silent church.

"My son, God will give you the wings of the morning, and you will reach people in minutes and hours where it would normally take days and weeks!" Then Shock returned to the platform, as if something this bizarre happened in every service. John sat there completely dazed, recalling two prophecies that had been given him in his teenage years.

"I don't know what God had in mind by that statement, young man," Shock offered from the pulpit, "but it was from God! Refuse to be discouraged—God is going to use you!"

John knew the prophecy could have only one meaning—he was going to have a missionary ministry with an airplane. But how? All he had was a shell of a plane in Monterrey. Was God going to send him back to Durango? Would Wings of a Dove change its mind? He heard little of the sermon as he thought of possible solutions, but he could hardly imagine what God would do. He knew that the only way he could return to the mission field was if he got the money to reconstruct his airplane. Somehow, it had to be done!

From that time on, he became obsessed with finding the money to repair the plane, getting it in the air, and beginning his work. He knew that working at the college would not provide adequate funds to repair the plane. He needed another job!

Several days later, the phone rang.

When Josie answered, the operator's nasal voice announced a long-distance call for "Mr. John Eye-uls."

John took the phone and waited through the crackling for the connection to be completed.

"Hi, John. Guess who this is!" The voice sounded familiar.

"I know you," John acknowledged, trying to attach a face to the voice. "I just can't place you at the moment."

"This is Joe Vlahovic in Kenosha, Wisconsin—your old hometown."

John instantly remembered the good times he'd had with Joe back at Lake Shore Tabernacle.

"Joe! What in the world are you doing these days?"

"I heard you were working at the college and was just wondering if you would like to move up here and make a fortune selling juices. I'm working for Milton Hess, who is the president of the Home Juice Company and a wonderful Christian."

"Strangely enough, I've been thinking about trying to find another job. Your call might be an answer to prayer."

"Why don't you and Josie come up to Kenosha, and we can attack the problem here?" Joe urged.

"Sounds great, Joe! I'd like to see everyone again, and I'm definitely interested in making more money!"

As soon as John hung up, Josie asked, "When do we leave?"

Grinning at his wife's eavesdropping, John said, "I'll talk to President Coote tomorrow. If he's willing, we'll leave within the week."

A week later, they were in Kenosha, where they received a warm welcome from the Vlahovic family. John immediately started working for Milton Hess. His enthusiasm began to rise as he began saving money to get his plane repaired.

They had been in Kenosha just a few weeks when John received a long-distance call from Sam McKenzie in Durango. John could hardly contain himself as he waited for the call to come through. Had Wings of a Dove changed its mind? Was Sam calling to tell him he was now part of the team? Could it be possible that he and Josie would soon be going back to Durango? He waited for what felt like a long time before he heard Sam's familiar voice at the other end of the line.

"How are you doing, John?" Sam asked.

"Fine, Sam!" John fired back ethusiastically. "It looks like I'm going to be able to get my plane in the air before too long!"

In the silence that followed, John waited to hear that he was needed and wanted in Durango.

"John, that's what I'm calling you about—the plane!"

"What about the plane?" John was puzzled.

"I just sold it to a man in Pharr, Texas."

John's mind went numb. Surely, his ears had heard wrong. Sam had sold his plane? Without even asking him? How could he do such a thing?

"What do you mean, Sam?"

"I knew you wouldn't be coming back to Durango, and this man came by and made an offer—so I just sold it. I'm mailing the title to you, and I'd appreciate it if you'd sign it and return it as soon as possible."

John was incredulous. The words he'd heard from the board official at Wings of a Dove returned to his mind as a monotonous refrain: "You're useless; you're a detriment. You're useless; you're a detriment." John heard himself agree to sign the title. He was in no mood to resist. Maybe he was useless after all.

This was the bottom—absolute rock bottom. John had yet to learn that the bottom is often the place where individuals find God.

TWELVE

THE RETURN

At Lake Shore Tabernacle the following Sunday morning, John felt alone, even though he was surrounded by people. Why was he experiencing such a reversal? Was God displeased with his life? Why had every ray of hope turned to darkness? The mission field had never seemed farther away than it did now.

After the service, Danny Vlahovic met him in the aisle and asked a question that pierced his heart: "Do you have an airplane, John?"

"Not right now. I'm looking around for a Taylorcraft." (A missionary had once told him that those planes were ideal for flying over rugged terrain.)

"What will it take to get you into such a plane?" Danny probed.

"Oh…" John rubbed his chin and ventured a wild guess: "Roughly one thousand dollars."

"You've got your airplane, John."

"What do you mean?"

"Wally Zelensky and I are going in together to put you back in the air. We feel that Mexico is God's place for you, and it's time for you to return!"

Within a few minutes, John was holding a thousand-dollar check in his hand, thanks to the generosity of two friends from Lake Shore Tabernacle.

He thought for sure it was a dream. In a little while, he'd wake up and discover the harsh reality of his miserable circumstances. But, no, he knew it wasn't a dream; it was really happening! He threw his arms around Danny and burst into laughter. "Oh, thank God!" he whooped. "Thank God!"

The following morning, John started his search for a Taylorcraft. To sharpen his flying skills, he rented a Cessna and combined plane-hunting with flying. His first refueling stop was at a tiny airport near Rockford, Illinois. As he walked into the office to request fuel, the man behind the desk initiated conversation with a startling question: "Would you like to buy a Taylorcraft airplane?"

John was almost too shocked to reply. Finally, he managed, "Yes, indeed, I would! Why do you ask?"

"It just so happens that I have one for sale."

"Let's see it!"

In the hangar, John discovered a 1944 L-2 tandem Taylorcraft, painted red and white, with the numerals N47205 gleaming on the side.

"Would it be possible for me to fly it?"

"Absolutely! Take off!"

Together they pushed the plane out of the hangar. John climbed into the cockpit and urged the mechanical bird into the blue sky. It was love at first flight. But how could he possibly buy this beautiful plane with the meager sum he had?

John landed and taxied the plane back to the hangar. Climbing out with as much nonchalance as he could muster, he popped the question both men were waiting for: "What do you want for this plane?"

"Sixteen hundred is a giveaway price. I have at least that much money in the ship!"

"I'll tell you what. I have a thousand dollars, and—"

"Then there is no need to talk anymore. A thousand dollars isn't an offer—it's an insult!"

John left, knowing he would return. He somehow sensed that this particular plane had been reserved for him. After several days, he phoned the owner long-distance. "I still have this thousand dollars. Do you have any other offers?"

"No, I don't have any other offers, but your bid is ridiculous. Tell you what—I'll come down to fifteen hundred. You go find another five hundred, and let's get together."

The conversation terminated without a change of position by either party. Nevertheless, John continued believing that the new-found plane was going to be his. It was his ticket back to Mexico— back to his ministry—back to where God wanted him to be.

Early the next morning, John instructed his faithful wife to get up and get dressed. Sleepily, Josie asked, "Why?"

"We're going to drive up to Rockford today and buy that plane!"

"But I thought you said last night that the man wanted fifteen hundred dollars for it!"

"That's right. But I believe God wants me to have that plane, and today we're going to go buy it—with this thousand-dollar check!"

"Oh. Well, a ride up there will be nice, anyway!"

On the way to Rockford, John pelted heaven with fervent prayer. "Lord, I'm ready to return to Mexico. If You want me to go back, please fix it so I can buy that plane with the money I have."

At the airport, the surprised owner of the plane greeted them with a hopeful question: "Did you find another five hundred dollars?"

"Nope," John replied. "I just came back to talk, with that same thousand dollars."

"Aw, look, pal—be reasonable!" The owner was pleading with hands extended. "I can't throw five hundred dollars away. There's just no way we can get together without more money involved!"

As they talked, the owner's brother arrived, driving a brand-new Cadillac convertible. While they were admiring the car, John got an idea.

"Be nice if you had a Cadillac like your brother," he remarked casually.

"Yeah, it sure would be! I just don't have the down payment right now." The man had set his own trap, and John baited it.

"If you sold the plane for a thousand dollars this morning, you could be driving your new Cadillac this afternoon!"

The man took the bait without a second thought. "I'll do it! You just bought yourself an airplane!"

John signed the necessary papers, jumped into the waiting Taylorcraft, and made his preparations to return to Kenosha by air. Josie drove back home alone, and the plane's erstwhile owner left for the Cadillac dealership.

~

On the flight back to Kenosha, John thanked God over and over for the miraculous turn of events that had secured him an airplane. Just a few days ago, his shell of an aircraft had been sold. Now the Lord had given him another plane twice as capable. What a wonderful God he served! John wasn't even worried about the other mode of transportation he needed to be supplied before he could return to Mexico—a car. That fabulous, faith-propelled Ford was a disaster waiting to happen. But God had provided an airplane, and John knew the car would come soon.

In a few days, John received an invitation to speak at a church in Fort Worth, Texas.

When John arrived at the church driving Old Faithful the Ford, the minister, Mr. Weaver, greeted him with, "Son, you need another car—bad!"

"Yes, I know," John admitted. "More than a year ago, Josie and I stopped just outside of El Centro, California, to pray for its screaming, smoking rear wheel. It's run perfectly ever since, but I know it will fall apart any day now. It's good only for the junkyard."

John's disarming honesty seemed to rouse Mr. Weaver's acquisitive instincts. He explained that his wife worked at a finance company, and whenever a car was returned or reposed, Weaver usually bought it, fixed it up, and sold it. "I know about cars, John," he said. "I've bought and sold them for years, so let me be the judge about this car—okay?"

"That's fine by me, but don't say you weren't warned," John cautioned him.

"I have a 1950 Plymouth, dark blue, that's in great condition," Weaver offered. "Just to help you out, I'll buy your car for one hundred dollars and let you have the Plymouth."

"You mean you're just going to give me the Plymouth?"

"That's right, and pay you a hundred dollars to boot! Then I'll take your old car, fix it up, and see what I can make off it."

"I don't know how to thank you!" John blurted out. He felt impelled to add, "You're sure you can do something with my Ford?"

"Like I said, let me worry about it."

John did just that. Before he left Fort Worth, he was the proud new owner of the Plymouth, and Weaver had legally adopted the

Ford. Weaver drove Old Faithful exactly one block before the transmission fell out onto the street with a *clunk*. Several attempts at repairing it proved futile. John's words became prophecy: The car was sold to a junkyard for twenty-five dollars.

God had kept the Ford together for as long as His man had need of it. Meanwhile, the Plymouth performed beautifully on the thousand-mile trip back to Kenosha, and John knew that the Lord was ready for him to return to Mexico.

⌒

Again, John and Josie found themselves saying good-bye to their dear friends, but it wasn't as hard this time. Their hearts were already in Mexico, with the people who were waiting for the gospel.

The couple drove to the airport together, then parted ways with prayers for each other's safety. John would fly the plane to McAllen, Texas, where Josie would meet him within the car. After crossing the border into Mexico, they would again part company until they reached their destination.

John had prepared for his cross-country trip with caution, knowing that the Taylorcraft held only twelve gallons of gas and could fly at a minimum speed of eighty-five miles per hour. The plane lacked a heater, and the cockpit became so cold that the water in his canteen froze by the time he landed to refuel just outside Chicago. Disturbed by the black sky and high winds, John checked the weather report at the airport flight center. The forecast was very favorable. Dismissing his fears, he examined the flight plan for the second leg of his journey, then took off again, headed south.

Less than an hour out of Chicago, he flew into a dark haze of smoke and snow. Since the plane was not equipped for instrument navigation, he was flying "by the seat of his pants." He stared intently into the grayish fog, trying to spot a landmark—some object to identify where he was. There was nothing. In a matter of minutes, he was completely lost.

His only hope was to slip under the fog and locate some highway on the ground. As he slowly lowered his altitude, the engine became more labored, the propeller more sluggish, and the plane less responsive to commands.

Intent on finding a hole in the fog, John forgot to observe the altimeter. Suddenly, out of the corner of his eye, he saw something flash past the cockpit. Startled, John looked up and saw an industrial chimney just ahead. Was he that low? A quick check of the altimeter confirmed his fear.

Yanking the joystick into his midriff with one hand, he pushed the throttle all the way in with the other, commanding the aircraft to gain altitude. It didn't. Something was terribly wrong! Suddenly he remembered the ice in his canteen and realized why the plane refused to respond: the wings were covered with ice, and the additional weight was pushing the plane lower and lower, like a giant band from the sky.

Within seconds, the sputtering engine filled the cockpit with the sound of death. John pulled the carburetor-heat knob all the way back, which should have warmed the intake air and prevented the formation of ice in the fuel system. Seconds seemed like hours as he waited for the engine's rough thrashing to settle into a more rhythmic flow. It didn't. It became rougher—more sluggish. The plane was losing altitude, despite his best efforts to prevent it. Instinctively, he knew that he was going to crash, but he also knew that God was watching.

Suddenly he saw what his eyes had been searching for—a break in the fog. He nudged the sluggish plane through the opening and leveled off just a few feet above the ground. Beneath him was a cornfield. He couldn't have hoped for a better place to land.

Forcing the nose of the ice-laden plane into the air, he let the tail drag in the dried cornstalks, slowing his speed. The weary plane finally smashed to the ground, the propeller slinging cornstalks and dried leaves in all directions. John felt the seat belt burn into him. Seconds later, it was over. The plane had stopped smack in the center of some farmer's corn patch. John was thankful to be alive, but he dreaded facing that farmer!

Releasing the seat belt, he stepped out into the cold, icy mist and examined the plane. Miraculously, it was intact! When the weather cleared, he could fly out of this cornfield. The wide swath the prop had already cut through the crops would make takeoff relatively easy.

John spotted the farmer's home and trudged toward it with a mixture of thankfulness and dread. Several dogs barked, announcing his coming, and the farmer met him on the porch with a rather suspicious "Who are you?"

"You're not going to believe this, but I'm a missionary on my way to Mexico, and I've just parked my plane in your corn patch."

"You did *what*?" the farmer inquired dubiously.

John slowly repeated his introduction as the farmer rubbed his stubby beard and stared at him in disbelief.

"Well, son," the farmer finally quavered, "I've heard a lot of tales in my time, but this has to be one of the best. Yes, sir, one of the very best!"

John apologized for the damage to the corn, but the farmer dismissed it, "Think nothing of it, young man, think nothing of it! There's nothing out there but dried cornstalks!" He laughed and slapped his knee. "Just think what a tale it will make when I go to town Saturday! The only thing that generally lands in a cornfield is a crow, but I've got a whole airplane roosting in my corn patch! Yes, sir, that's worth telling about!"

Thankful the farmer found the situation amusing, John hesitatingly asked for a ride to the nearest motel. This the farmer graciously supplied, in spite of the bad weather.

The next morning, the sky was resplendent, with no cloud in sight. John returned to the farmer's field and examined his airplane once more. It seemed fit for flight. The brilliant sun had melted the ice from the wings and body. The engine started with no trouble and soon purred with perfection.

John turned the plane around and aimed it down the swath his propeller had cleared the night before. He revved the engine to the maximum, to get the quickest takeoff possible. The farmer, smiling and looking proud, stood and waved as the plane lurched forward, breaking the bonds of gravity and even more cornstalks.

The remainder of the flight went without mishap. John met Josie at the border right on schedule. After crossing, they continued their journey toward Monterrey, Mexico.

THIRTEEN

CAN GOD DO IT?

After their unexpectedly prolonged stay in the United States, John and Josie needed several months of concentrated study in Monterrey to regain fluency in Spanish. Afterward, when they finally moved to Victoria, John felt he was ready to preach to the Mexicans in their own language. He almost memorized his first sermon, which he delivered before a small church in the Huizachal Valley.

He held his congregants' attention with an imaginary story about a young mountain bird named George. George's parents had instructed him not to fly around by himself, because he could get into serious trouble. One day, after his parents left for work, George disobeyed. He flew to a river, where he landed on an ice-covered log floating on the water. The log was sprinkled with meat. As George ate the luscious meat, his forest friends on the river-bank warned him that there was a waterfall just around the bend, but George cockily reminded them that he was a bird and could fly away from danger at any time—not so unlike many of us when we do not take the danger of sin seriously!

When John approached the climax of his story, the tone took an unexpected turn. The Spanish word for "animal foot," or "paw," is *pata*, while the word for "duck" is *pato*. A slight difference in sound; a great difference in meaning. John continued, "Suddenly, George saw the waterfall just ahead, and he tried to fly off the ice-covered log, but he could not. Do you know why?"

The rapt audience responded lustily, "No! Why?"

"Because his ducks were frozen to the log!"

The villagers broke out in side-bursting laughter. John was shattered. Days of effort had gone into writing and memorizing this very serious story, with the prayerful intent that some would be converted—not convulsed. It was all he could do to force a smile when the congregation very patiently explained his linguistic error.

On his way home that afternoon, John was flagged down by a sombrero-topped, dust-covered traveler who asked, "Are you Brother John?"

"Yes, I am. What can I do for you?"

"We've heard that you have come to our area to preach the gospel of Jesus Christ. Would you please come to the village of La Reforma? We've never heard this gospel. Please, please come, amigo!"

John agreed to come that night, and the villager gave him a crude map to guide him through the glorified goat trails that connected one remote Mexican village to another. As he traveled to La Reforma for the service that night, John often had to get out of his vehicle, roll up his trousers, push his way out of knee-deep mud, or cut away overgrowth with a hatchet before he could proceed. The journey took several hours, and he was exhausted and plastered with mud when he arrived. He found the congregation waiting patiently in a little room filled with backless plank benches. A dog was curled up under the front bench, and several children who had fallen asleep while awaiting his arrival were lying on the floor.

A mother in the rear of the church was breast-feeding her infant. This was Mexico.

John slung his guitar over his shoulder and began teaching the people some gospel choruses. As he sang, he felt something crawling on his muddy legs. Looking down, he saw that they were covered with fleas. He wanted to brush them off, but he wondered what his audience would think. Their children were sleeping on the floor where those fleas were coming from! He gritted his teeth and kept singing, stamping his feet to the rhythm.

After the song session, in which the congregation had participated with enthusiasm, he shared a simple message that Jesus Christ is God and that He can both save and heal. At the end of the sermon, the village alcalde came forward and said to him, before the whole congregation, "You have told us that Jesus Christ can heal. Are you sure?"

"Yes, I'm very sure," John replied.

"Then come with me." He led John out of the church and through the village to an abandoned warehouse. The entire congregation followed but did not ask questions. Mexican people tell you what they want you to know when they want you to know it.

As they entered the musty warehouse, the alcalde took an ancient kerosene lantern from the wall and lit it, illuminating an object huddled in a corner. At first, John thought it was an animal. Then he realized it was a human being—a young man about twenty-five years of age, covered with dirt and clothed in tattered rags.

The alcalde spoke again, his voice echoing in the empty room: "You said God could heal. This man came up here from the valley. He's insane."

There was silence while John prayed for guidance. The alcalde asked impatiently, "Can God do it? We're all friends of his. Can God actually heal this man?"

"Yes, God can do it!" John replied with conviction. "How did he get into this condition?"

"He wanted to marry a young girl," the alcalde replied, "but she didn't like him. She went to a *curandero*,[9] and that very day, his mind left him. He roams the mountains like a wild animal, not knowing his name or the names of his family members and friends. If God heals—heal him!"

John looked at the circle of faces reflecting the dim light of the lantern. He and God were on the spot. If this man wasn't healed, the gospel would never be accepted in La Reforma. Knowing this was a case of demon possession, John prayed in the authority of Jesus' name for the young man to be released from the evil spirit. The prayer was short and very simple. He had hardly finished when the man spoke the first coherent words he had uttered in five years: "I'm tired!"

"Let him sleep," the alcalde said. "When he wakes tomorrow, we will know if God can heal. Come for services again tomorrow night, Brother John!"

The following night, driving his mud machine, John approached the house where the service was to be held. He found it surrounded by people. When the village leader spotted John's vehicle, he raced toward it, screaming, "God did it! God did it! God did it!"

"What happened?" John yelled, trying to make himself heard over the clamor of excited voices.

"This morning when that young man woke up, he came to my house and…and he called my whole family by name!" The alcalde stopped to wipe away the tears that flowed down his cheeks, then continued, "This he has not done for years. Today he is a different boy. God can do it! God can do it! Let's hear more about this gospel of Jesus Christ!"

---

9. *curandero*: witch doctor.

Thirty-five villagers were converted that night. John's miracle ministry had begun.

After holding several more services in La Reforma, John invited the new converts to experience the baptism in the Holy Spirit. Many were instantly filled. The most spectacular case was that of Lenora, whose life had been so completely changed since her conversion that many thought her to literally be a new person. An hour after receiving the baptism in the Holy Spirit and the gift of tongues, she stood, face glowing, and asked John to allow her to speak to the people. John agreed, not knowing what was coming.

Lenora began, "I've just seen a picture show, and I was in it. I was going down this beautiful green path with trees on both sides, and in the middle of this path was a white pigeon. It flew to me and sat on my head. When it did, I felt like a warm spring was flowing out of my heart, and I began speaking with a new language."

Not knowing what a vision was, she called it a "picture show"; not knowing that a dove was symbolic of the Holy Spirit, she called it a "pigeon." Nonetheless, her communication was perfect. Many followed her in receiving the Holy Spirit baptism. The fellowship that was established in La Reforma is still thriving, and the good news is penetrating the surrounding wilderness.

The news that a certain Brother John had brought a miracle-working gospel to the villages surrounding Victoria spread like a fire in a dry prairie. Requests for ministry came from everywhere. Many people walked for miles and even days to ask—to beg, if necessary—for the gospel to be shared in their desolate villages.

John went to Tamatan next. Within two weeks, more than a hundred villagers were attending glorious worship services marked by supernatural manifestations. The fervor of the new Christians there soon aroused aggressive opposition from a nearby church that professed to be Christian but did not preach the gospel of Jesus Christ. Some of its church members accused John of belonging to

Satan, and they demanded that the villagers stay away from his services. Even more people went to see what was going on.

Then the church tried a more subtle approach. For three months, it conducted a daily raffle in the lot adjacent to the building where John was holding worship services. Free food and clothing were dispensed lavishly in a wild, carnivalesque atmosphere. The people in Tamatan were miserably poor and worked like Pharaoh's slaves to keep food on their tables and clothes on their backs. John lost a handful of congregants to the other church and its raffle.

The remainder of his congregants, resisting the temptation to accept something that would provide only temporarily satisfaction for their flesh, continued feasting on the true Bread that John offered. After three months, when the supply of free food and clothes was exhausted, God was just warming up.

The third attack was more violent than the first two, and more effective. The leaders of the opposing church issued a decree that anyone who attended John's services would have his home burnt to the ground. At his next service, John looked into the troubled faces of five lonely Mexicans who were willing to sacrifice everything they owned to hear the gospel just one more time.

The small band of beleaguered believers united in prayer for God to intervene on behalf of His gospel. While they were praying, God was answering. A woman named Rosa came to the service that night with a dying baby in her arms. Standing before John in a tattered dress, her dark hair hanging in disarray, she searched his eyes.

"I don't believe in what you teach. But the doctor has said my baby will die tonight. Her blood is diseased." She paused to wipe a fly from the baby's pallid cheek. Then she continued, "I'm desperate—very desperate. If Jesus Christ can heal this baby, everyone in this village will know that His gospel is indeed the truth. Everyone knows the baby is dying, and no one can help—no one."

John took the baby in his arms and asked the Father, in the name of Jesus, to heal her. The child seemed almost lifeless when he handed her back to the weeping mother. But as John made his way home that night, he received an assurance that God had worked a miracle for the glory of His gospel. The work at Tamatan would not perish. Though God's church was persecuted, it would prosper—and soon.

When John returned to the church the following night, he found the meeting place packed with jubilant Mexicans. After he pushed himself inside, Rosa greeted him with eyes brimming with tears and held out the baby for him to see. He hardly recognized the child. Her pallor was gone, and she was the picture of health.

Before the whole congregation, Rosa told him, "Last night, my baby was dying when I came for prayer. Today, she is alive and well. I don't understand your gospel, Brother John, but it has worked a miracle. I went to every house in this village and told the people what God's power has done. They have come tonight to see and hear more about Jesus."

The revival had begun! No carnival, threat, or accusation could stop the tidal wave of spiritual renewal. At the end of the service, the village alcalde stood and shared a testimony that would lead to the building of the first of many mission church buildings in that part of Mexico. "I'm sixty-five years old and have never seen a miracle in the church I've attended—not ever," he said. "I suggest we build a new church to teach the gospel of Jesus Christ."

There were fifty-five men in the village who were eligible to vote, and all of them were present at that service. When the vote was taken to decide whether to construct a new church building, it was fifty-three to two in favor of the project.

Actually, two churches were built—one in La Reforma and one in Tamatan—and the method of construction used for those churches set the precedent for many mission churches to follow.

John agreed to furnish the materials if the members would supply the labor. The cost of materials for building a nice adobe church was about one thousand dollars, and the money came—promptly and miraculously—from America.

Construction began by cutting down trees for the corner posts and roof beams. After large trees had been sunk into the ground at the four corners of the future building, smaller saplings of the same height were plunged deep into the soil every two feet. Twigs woven horizontally between the saplings made a mat into which the adobe clay was pressed, creating a wall. After the roof beams had been raised, they were laced with thin strips of wood to which palm branches were tied to make a waterproof shelter. After the adobe walls dried, they were whitewashed. Before long, the finished structure was the most impressive building in the village.

In Tamatan, getting water to the construction site was problematic. The spring was more than half a mile from the church, on the other side of a steep hill. Several hundred gallons of water were required for each day's clay quota. The women of the village met the challenge with amazing strength and stamina, carrying five gallons of water on their heads each trip without spilling a drop. Five- and six-year-old girls carried one-gallon buckets with equal efficiency. Some of the women carried water for as long as ten hours a day, until their feet were bloody, bruised, and swollen, and their hands chapped and raw.

At last, the two churches were finished. The Sunday dedication services were triumphant affairs, each one followed by a feast consisting of barbecued jackrabbit and other Mexican delicacies. The churches at Tamatan and La Reforma are places where God's presence and power still manifest in majesty and miracles.

John's next mission church was prayed into existence by a Mexican couple living in La Gloria, a small village just eight miles from the city limits of Victoria. John had often passed through there and wanted to bring the gospel to the residents as soon as he could. One Saturday afternoon, he simply walked through the village, handing out the same gospel tracts he dropped from the plane.

The villagers politely took the tracts as John went from house to house—or, rather, from yard to yard. A gringo was a rarity in that remote village, and curiosity brought people out of their homes. They stood behind their stake fences and reached out their hands for whatever this American was giving away.

At one home, John placed a tract in a man's hand and explained, "This is a story about a man named Jesus Christ. I want you to read it, and then, in a few days, I'll return and explain it to you." At that, the man's wife burst into tears.

"Why is she crying?" John asked her husband.

"She's crying for joy!"

"What's she so overjoyed about?" John probed.

"Thirteen years ago, my wife and I accepted Jesus Christ at a gospel meeting in Matamoros. Every day for thirteen years, we have been praying for someone to come preach Jesus to our village. It's taken so long—so long—but at last, you've come!" And the man began weeping, too.

With the help of this couple, Mr. and Mrs. Bernardo, John arranged to hold a service in the largest house of the village, which belonged to a *mariachi*[10] named Santos. At the appointed time, the entire population of the village—eighty souls—gathered there to see what was going to happen. The pattern that had developed at La Reforma and Tamatan continued: simple teaching of the Scripture, followed by a spiritual harvest and miraculous manifestations.

Within weeks, the majority of the citizens of La Gloria had accepted Jesus Christ, and soon another church building was

10. *mariachi*: a member of a Mexican street band.

constructed. This one had a concrete floor and actual walls. To the poverty-stricken villagers, it looked like a cathedral.

The first convert to receive the baptism in the Holy Spirit was a dark-skinned young Mexican named Andres. As John was praying with him before the whole congregation, Andres suddenly began speaking in a miraculous, flowing language that was unknown to him. The church members were not disturbed by the event. However, when Andres' dark face began glowing with a supernatural light until it was as white as John's, the church emptied in less than a minute.

When Andres went home several hours later, his face was still glowing. He was forced to sleep on the porch because his parents locked the door, frightened by the miraculous manifestation. The next morning, Andres' complexion had returned to its natural dark color, and he was invited back inside.

Andres is one of seven ministers from the small village of La Gloria who now trudges through the mountains of Mexico proclaiming the good news that transforms human lives.

FOURTEEN

DECLARE HIS WONDERS

Even John marveled at the undeniable miracles that took place from time to time. One of the most impressive instances of God's supernatural protection occurred in a little village about ninety miles south of Victoria. An aged man from this town had walked for days to find John and urge him to come conduct church services there.

Moved by the man's hunger for God and concern for his people, John promised to make the trip when the first chance arose. Then he added, "Tell you what—I'll drop gospel tracts over your city from my airplane this coming Sunday afternoon. Tell your people to read those tracts, and I'll come to conduct services."

"Thank you, Brother John!" the man responded. "Thank you so very much! We'll look for your plane this Sunday!"

Following the morning services in Victoria, John picked up several hundred tracts and drove to the airport. It was a beautiful day for flying, and he was glad he had a good reason to give the Taylorcraft some much-needed exercise after climbing to a comfortable altitude, he leveled off for the trip and settled back to enjoy the breathtaking view. The green wilderness was so beautiful and the sky so serene that he felt almost as if he could reach out and touch the face of God. The only thing that was missing was his old buddy Jerry, who had gone to the IBC for Bible training. Dear Jerry! How John missed him.

Spotting smoke from the village immediately ahead, he positioned the gospel tracts so that they were ready to be hurled out the window at the right moment. As the plane approached the village, he could see the streets dotted with excited Mexicans who must have heard his plane a long way off in the silence of the jungle.

As a precautionary measure, he made one preliminary pass over the village to check for any violent winds at the low altitude. Conditions seemed perfect for the second pass and gospel-drop.

Gaining altitude, John circled the village to position the plane for a perfect pass. Instinctively, he checked the area again for any signs of whirlwinds, or "dust devils," at ground level. Such winds could develop into twisters instantly, with enough force to smash the plane like a penny matchbox in the hands of a giant. But there were no signs of danger.

As he glided down toward the village again, with the engine throttled back, he could still see the villagers below, jumping, waving, and running in circles. Just as he reached for the gospel tracts he had placed on the instrument panel, he lost control of the plane. Instinct and training told him he had hit the top of a dust devil. The cockpit was filled with fluttering gospel tracts; full and partially emptied oil cans bounced off the walls.

As he struggled to regain control of the plane, the propeller suddenly stopped—without reason or explanation. The plane had no electrical starter, and his airspeed was too slow for the wind to turn the propeller. The plane was falling like a fatally wounded bird. Death was coming. Closing his eyes, John prayed that the plane would clear the village before crashing.

Then, for no reason, the engine started, and the plane lifted straight in the air, climbing to a lifesaving altitude. Powerfully and smoothly, the prop churned the air, taking the plane safely over the thatched roofs of the village. It was another miracle.

Within moments, John had completely regained control. He lifted a stray oil can from his lap and brushed the disheveled tracts from the instrument panel as he headed home. The Mexicans would be disappointed, but with death looming over their village, he decided to return later.

The subsequent Friday, he received a letter via airmail from Richard Harmon in Fort Wayne, Indiana, more than two thousand miles away. As John read the letter, he felt the hair rise on the back of his neck.

> Brother John,
>
> The strangest thing happened Sunday afternoon at the church prayer meeting. A sixteen-year-old girl stood as though she had been yanked to her feet and absolutely demanded that everyone begin praying immediately for a man named John who had been in our church in the past. (She doesn't know you.) You're the only John who has been in our church for some time. We're all wondering where you were last Sunday about two thirty our time—and if you were in any serious trouble....

John didn't have to compare the times. He knew that the very moment those Spirit-led Christians in Fort Wayne had begun praying, invisible hands had picked his airplane straight up and restarted the engine instantly. He was glad that those believers hadn't asked the girl to sit down so that they could take an offering, recognize a visitor, vote on an officer, or appoint a committee. Instead, they had prayed to the One who rules the world, and their prayers had saved John's life.

⌒

Soon afterward, while John was holding services in a remote village called Los Angeles, a man named Chon came to him and urged him to visit his home village. Los Angeles itself was in the wilderness—a grueling three-hour drive from Victoria—and John wondered where this man had come from.

"Where is your village?" John asked Chon.

"Three hours in that direction." He pointed south.

"There aren't even trails in that direction. How are we going to get to your village, Chon?"

"We walk, señor," the Mexican replied dryly, as if the answer should have been known before the question had been asked.

"How did you hear about the gospel I am preaching?" John wanted to know.

Chon proceeded to tell a deeply moving story. "Eighteen years ago, a woman rode into our village with a pump organ mounted on two donkeys. She came from nowhere, left, and has never returned. She taught us one time about Jesus Christ, and the whole village accepted Him. We have worshipped Him for eighteen years, waiting for someone else to come with more about this great story."

John felt tears brim in his eyes. Eighteen years of faithfulness to a Savior whose gospel they scarcely knew!

"How many are in your village?" John questioned.

"Twenty-eight," Chon fired back proudly, as if the statistic were staggering. Waiting for John to commit himself, Chon presented his request again. "Brother John, please come! I know it's a long way—three hours in and three hours out—but I will walk with you every step. Each time you are in Los Angeles, I will come here and lead you to my people. I will have to walk twelve hours; you will have to walk only six."

John needed no further prodding; he was simply trying to gain control of his emotions. Finally, he was able to talk. "Yes, Chon, I'll come to your village. I'd be honored to meet your people and teach them more of the Bible."

John invited Felix, a native evangelist, to come along. Their three-hour walk took them through the deepest bush John had ever seen. Chon nimbly picked his way through tiny breaks in the foliage, his legs like two knitting needles weaving a complicated pattern. At times, the men had to hack their way through the bush with machetes, always pressing in the general direction Chon knew by instinct. The undergrowth was sometimes so dense that the sun was hidden from view.

At last, the three of them arrived at Chon's village—a hamlet so small and so remote that it did not have a name. The small circle of thatched houses constituted a circle of innocence, untouched by violence or fear. There had been no robbery, theft, or other criminal activity in that village for eighteen years. No personal conflicts demanded the attention of the village president; it was a community without strife. John had never visited such a place. Surely heaven would be a little like this—a place where all were loved, honored, and respected. As soon as he and Chon broke through the last veil of foliage, the villagers stepped out of their humble huts and came to greet them one at a time. This was a momentous occasion indeed. A visitor was a rare thing, and a visitor who could tell them more about Jesus was like an angel from heaven.

After greeting the entire population of the village, John and Felix entered Chon's tiny adobe hut. It was full of goats—the heating system of rural Mexican villages. The odor was overwhelming, but it did not bother anyone except John. A complete sinus block would have been a blessing right then!

After conducting a service that combined worship with teaching, John and Felix offered to pray with anyone who had a special need. A three-year-old girl was brought forward; she had a spinal disorder that forced her to bend forward almost ninety degrees.

John could see the expectancy on the people's faces. He prayed on simple prayer—and one mighty miracle resulted. As the little girl popped straight up, tears of joy flowed down the face of everyone present. A feeling of awesome reverence filled the house where they sat, and the Spirit of the Almighty was upon them all.

For two years, John conducted services in this nameless community. Every two weeks when he came to Los Angeles, Chon would walk through the jungle to meet him and lead him to the village. The next day, he would accompany John back to Los Angeles and then begin the three-hour walk back home alone. John wondered if such faithfulness could be matched by anyone on the globe, and he thanked God for calling him to minister to these people.

⌒

The church at Rancho Nuevo was one of the first and most stable of the mission churches John had established. The villagers had cut out a landing strip in the jungle for Brother John's plane, and he held services there once a week.

Just after he had landed in Rancho Nuevo one fall afternoon, a woman ran to his plane while the propeller was still spinning— something he had cautioned the people not to do. Ignoring the danger of being hacked to shreds, she forcibly opened the door to the cockpit and began pulling John out before he had even released his seat belt. As she tugged at him, she cried hysterically, "Brother John, I must have help! I must have help!"

John recognized the woman as Isabella, a member of his church whose health had been prayed for many times but who never seemed to get better. This afternoon, she and her husband escorted John into their humble home and bolted the door shut behind him.

"I don't want you to think I'm crazy," she began, "but something very strange has been happening to me lately. I see this very bright image coming toward me—so bright, I can hardly look at it!"

"Does it speak to you?" John asked.

"Yes—yes, it does speak to me."

"What does it say?"

"It says that I must worship it; that it has more power than Jesus Christ; and that if I would adore it, I would be healed instantly."

John recognized the problem immediately.

"This power is an evil spirit," he told Isabella. "It's not of God but of the devil. Don't you remember how I taught you about the devil trying to get Jesus to fall down and worship him in the wilderness?"

"Has someone tried to curse me with black magic?" she asked fearfully.

"That's possible. However, the Scriptures say that we have complete authority over the devil and his demon spirits, in the name of Jesus. If you and your husband are willing to fast and pray for ten days, I'll fast, too. At the end of that time, I'll come back to your home to seek God's deliverance for you."

The couple agreed to join him in the ten-day fast. The Lord often gave John the ability to fast for long periods of time. Even though he abstained from all food and drink (except water) during these fasts, his physical strength was maintained, and he continued ministering as usual.

After the fast, John returned to Rancho Nuevo. Again, Isabella met his plane before the propeller had stopped spinning and tried to drag him out the door. This time, however, her face was radiant.

"I'm healed, Brother John, I'm completely healed! For the first time in my life, I'm perfectly well!"

"Tell me what happened, Isabella."

"Eight days after our fast, the bright image returned to my house. It appeared over the fireplace in the kitchen, and this time my husband saw it, too."

"What did you do?"

"My husband took my hand, and we prayed together, using these words: 'In the name of Jesus Christ, we command you to leave this house immediately!'"

"What happened then?" John was finding it hard to maintain his professional calm.

"The bright image stopped talking instantly. Then we both knew we had power over it, so we repeated our prayer again, only this time much louder—much, much louder!"

"And then what?"

"Well, the strangest thing—as we kept taking authority over it in the name of Jesus, the brightness of the image grew dimmer, like a lamp about to run out of oil. Finally, it just faded out completely."

"That's a miracle!" John declared.

"The wonderful thing is that, as soon as the light went out, I was instantly healed! A warm feeling covered my whole body, and I knew I was completely well."

Isabella's husband took up the story at this point. "Yes, she went to every house in the village, screaming that she was healed, and that Jesus Christ had done it. We've never been attacked by evil spirits before, but now we know we have the power in Christ to defeat them. We'll never be afraid of black magic again."

FIFTEEN

FAREWELL TO JERRY

John was in California, paying a long-overdue visit to some of the churches that contributed to his mission work. After speaking at a church in Sacramento on Sunday night, he visited the pastor's family at the parsonage. The laughter that filled the house as he recounted some of his unusual experiences in the mission field almost drowned out the ring of the telephone in the adjoining room.

The pastor's wife went to answer it, then quickly returned and told John that he had a long-distance call. "It's from Josie's sister, Joyce Mullings," she said.

John excused himself, went into the next room, and took the phone. With laughter still in his voice, he said, "Hello, Joyce! What are you up to this time of night?"

"John, I'm afraid I have some terribly bad news for you. It's about Jerry Witt."

John sobered instantly. "What's the matter with Jerry?"

"John, I'm very sorry to have to be the one to tell you, but Jerry has been killed in a plane accident."

John's stomach knotted as if kicked by a horse, and for a moment, he was unable to speak. Jerry had recently graduated from the IBC and had returned to Mexico to resume his gospel "bombing raids." Finally, John's stammering lips formed the words, "Jerry? Dead? It's impossible! Who told you?"

"President Coote called yesterday and asked me to forward the message to you. He didn't know where to reach you."

"Where is Jerry's body now?"

"Evidently his body is still with the wreckage in the mountains. All reports indicate that the plane is completely charred. You know what that means."

"Yes, I know what it means." John's brain went numb as shock and grief settled over him like a heavy blanket dropped from the ceiling. After a long silence, he finally managed to ask, "Where will the funeral be held?"

"Revival Temple in San Antonio. Jerry's father is out of the country, so President Coote has gone to Mexico to claim the body."

"Thank you for calling, Joyce. The news was bad, but it had to come. I'll see you in San Antonio."

John had made the trip from Southern California to San Antonio many times in the past ten years, but never had it seemed to take so long. Memories of Jerry flooded his mind, and with each remembrance came a new rush of tears for his fallen friend. It seemed only yesterday they were standing at the airport watching the Flying Tigers use a rope to start the DC-3 engines. Since then, how many flying hours had he and Jerry logged together, and how many villages had they "bombed" with gospel tracts? For a moment, his grief was forgotten as he remembered the trip that had almost ended with imprisonment.

John kept waiting for this horrible dream to end. It didn't, however, and he realized that it never would when he entered Revival Temple and saw the closed casket submerged in scarlet flowers.

The sanctuary was packed with students from International Bible College and missionaries from all ports of call, most of whom had been trained at IBC. A family of Christian believers had come home to say farewell to a dedicated servant of the One whom they also served. President Coote's tribute to Jerry was delivered in a voice deep with emotion. Like the brief committal service at Mission Burial Cemetery, it was charged with a note of victory and assurance. Why Jerry's earthly life—so full of promise and so totally dedicated to the Master's service—had been snuffed out so early was beyond human understanding; exactly how he'd been killed also remained a mystery. Only one thing was certain: Jerry himself was not in that casket but was now with his Lord, receiving the reward of a *"good and faithful servant"* (Matthew 25:21, 23).

After the service, John spent a few days on the IBC campus, trying to find some *"balm in Gilead"* (Jeremiah 8:22) to heal his heartache and struggling to conquer the growing fear that had seized him when he heard of Jerry's death—he would be next. His plane was much older than Jerry's, far less powerful, and far more susceptible to the treacherous mountain downdrafts. Jerry had often told him that if either of them was ever killed in a crash, it would be John in his ancient T-craft.

As John walked onto the campus, he was stopped by Mrs. Schrader, President Coote's mother-in-law, who was known throughout the state of Texas for her powerful ministry of prevailing prayer. John was delighted to see her.

"I have a word from the Lord for you, John," she said without preamble.

"I'm delighted to hear that. What is it?"

"I had a vision last night that concerned you. I saw these three things: a beautiful white flower blooming with radiant life, a gnarled little oak tree, and a Gardener whose countenance shone with glory. The Gardener picked the flower in the peak of its bloom. He didn't explain why; it was His garden, and He chose to take it. The gnarled oak was left standing."

"But what part of this vision related to me?"

"John, you are the oak tree left to serve; Jerry was the beautiful flower plucked by our Lord at a time of His choosing." She paused, then continued, "The Scripture that I'm about to give you came to me because the Holy Spirit has told me you are very fearful of returning to Mexico's mountains in your airplane."

"You are absolutely right," John confirmed. "The fear has been with me constantly since I heard the news about Jerry."

"The Scripture is this—and I believe it applies to you: '*He found him in a desert land…; he led him about, he instructed him, he kept him as the apple of his eye.…So the* Lord *alone did lead him.… He made him ride on the high places of the earth*' (Deuteronomy 32:10, 12–13). Brother John, you will return to Mexico and fly again for His glory and gospel!"

John knew she was right. While she talked, the gnawing fear lifted, and peace settled on him like a dove. He would return to Mexico immediately and do what he'd feared he would never have the courage to do: personally examine the crash scene to see where his dear friend's life had been snuffed out.

⁓

Jerry's plane had crashed on a mountainside near the village of Las Coloradas. John stood at the site of the accident, plotting out in his mind the route Jerry must have taken in order to drop gospels on the tiny village nestled in the deep valley.

John saw the huge mountain standing like a monstrous backstop behind a two-hundred-foot rocky ridge. The ridge created a blind canyon, which would have been imperceptible to a pilot flying north until it was too late.

John knew that Jerry, after having "bombed" the village, must have banked the plane to the left; a pilot instinctively turns a plane to his own side, where he has greater visibility. But that had been his fatal move. With the box canyon just before him, the strong and continuous stream of air rolling down the backstop mountain had literally blown Jerry's plane into the mountainside.

Around the three-foot hole where the engine had struck the rocky soil, twisted and charred pieces of steel stood up from the ground in grotesque configurations. The death scene was burned into John's brain. He knew at that moment that he must replace the exhausted and underpowered Taylorcraft, or he would be next. What he did not know was that God was already working to supply this need.

Soon after John returned to Victoria, he received a call from Charles Diffee, a minister at one of his supporting churches in Dallas. After expressing his sympathy to John, Pastor Diffee stated, "I'm personally against your flying, John, but if you insist on continuing it, come to Dallas and let me help you find a good airplane."

John gratefully accepted his invitation, and the next day, he flew to Dallas in the Taylorcraft. He hoped to buy a Cessna 182—a four-seater aircraft with a 230-horsepower engine. He knew that a used plane of this type would cost about twelve thousand dollars, which might as well have been twelve million. However, he also knew he could not underestimate God's ability or willingness to supply.

In Dallas, John and Pastor Diffee went to see Jay Cole, a Baptist layman who owned an airplane dealership. Sitting in front of his office was a shimmery green-and-white Cessna. Recognizing John's interest in the plane, Jay asked, "How do you like it?"

"That's real nice! What do you want for it?"

"Ninety-six hundred."

John whistled, then smiled at Jay's expression. "The price isn't that bad, Jay; I just don't have that much money for a plane!"

"I'll give you sixteen hundred on your plane, John, and we can—"

"Look, Jay, from one friend to another, this plane of mine has had it. I don't think it's worth a dime more than three hundred."

"I'll take that chance. Let's see—that leaves you with a balance of eight thousand. What do you think?"

"Not a bad deal at all, but I'll have to finance this plane; and on my income, it will demand a major miracle and a very flexible banker!"

"Why so flexible?" Jay asked.

"Who wants to finance a plane that's going across the border into Mexico?"

"Oh, I see. Well, think it over and come back if you can find that miracle banker!"

John and Diffee walked to the car in silence.

As they got in the car, Pastor Diffee said, "Let's go find some money. I've received good service from the National Bank on Buckner Boulevard. They're very aggressive and unusually considerate."

John laughed out loud. "Man, that's what we need—someone very, very aggressive and very, very considerate!"

They entered the bank and conversed with the loan officer about John's missionary activities. He seemed to take a great interest in the versatile plane ministry. "Tell you what," he said. "I've got a plane for you to see. If you buy it from me, the financing will not be a problem."

When John saw the plane, he knew instantly that he didn't want a thing to do with it. It was a carbon copy of Jerry's plane.

Suddenly feeling sick, he made quick apologies and abruptly terminated the bargaining session.

Three additional days of plane-shopping throughout the Southwest produced nothing. The path led right back to Jay Cole and the powerful Cessna 182 that was still sitting in front of his office. The bright green numerals—N5476B—stood out sharply against the white background. When Jay saw John and Pastor Diffee, he came out smiling. His salesman's instinct told him John was hooked.

"John, it's obvious that you want this plane, or you wouldn't be back staring at it as if you'd been hypnotized."

"You're right, Jay. I do want it, but eight thousand is still out of my reach."

"Tell you what, John—I'll take the radio and oxygen equipment out, and that will knock the price down to the bone. Just seven thousand and your old plane. You can't pass that up—no way!"

"You're right! It's a deal!" Looking at Diffee, John said, "Let's go back and talk to that banker. I hope he feels as good today as he felt four days ago. Seven thousand is a lot to risk in Mexico."

"I wonder how he'd feel about financing an airplane bought from someone else."

"Let's go find out!"

Twenty minutes later, they were seated before the giant walnut desk of the loan officer. John blurted out, "I want to finance a plane, but not your plane."

"Well, there's nothing like coming to the point," the bank executive replied good-humoredly. He opened his desk and located his rate book. "Let's see what financing possibilities we can offer."

John waited. He knew the banker had no idea what kind of "possibilities" he would be able to offer before this deal could be closed.

"All right. Since you are a missionary, we'll give you a break. Your monthly payments will be two hundred fifty. How's that?" The loan officer smiled at John as if he expected him to jump for joy.

He didn't even grin. "That's way too much!"

At that point, the loan officer lost his smile, as well. He cleared his throat before making a counter offer. "How would two twenty-five suit you?"

"That's still a little stiff."

The loan officer's face became grimmer. "How about two hundred?"

"No—no, I can't!"

"Would one seventy-five be too much?" He seemed to be pleading.

"Let's get it a little lower if we can," John countered.

"Why don't we go get some coffee? Then maybe—just maybe—we can reach an agreement!" The loan officer led the way to the coffee shop.

Ten minutes later, they returned to battle. John opened with a broadside: "I'll be honest and tell you that I have just two hundred and fifty dollars a month pledged to me at this time."

The patient banker asked in desperation, "John, what can you pay? Surprise me!" He had asked for it, and John wouldn't disappoint him.

"How about eighty dollars a month?" He said it without flinching. Pastor Diffee nearly fell to the floor.

The loan officer gasped. "You surprised me, all right!" There was a tense silence, and then the banker said, "Believe me, this is highly irregular—correction: almost insane—but we'll do it!"

One week later, John was flying his nine-thousand-dollar Cessna 182 back to the bush of Mexico.

SIXTEEN

GOD BUYS A FARM

Having seen the impossibility of single-handedly reaching the thousands upon thousands of people who were clamoring for the gospel, John purchased a one-acre plot twelve miles north of Victoria to begin a Bible school that would train qualified villagers who wanted to enter the ministry. Since the students would come from impoverished families, the school would have to be self-supporting.

In a matter of weeks, the property was overrun with two cows, five pigs, fifty chickens, and millions of bees in more than a hundred hives. John named the school "The Nest of the Eagles," since Bible schools are illegal in Mexico.

The Nest of the Eagles had just opened when Pastor Gene Sattler from Marthaville, Louisiana, paid a visit. Before leaving, he gave John some advice: "John, you're boxed in on this overcrowded acre. You need to step out on faith!"

"You're telling me to step out on faith?" John repeated.

"Yes indeed, I am!"

"But I'm spending more than seventy-five dollars a day now, and we have less than twenty dollars a day pledged to our ministry.

I have to pray in the difference to support our school, the native pastors, and their churches. What am I stepping out on, if it's not faith?"

Pastor Sattler did not reply, and the matter was not discussed again. John, however, did not forget the conversation.

A few weeks passed. One morning, John was greeted warmly in the plaza by a friend named Jesús Rodriguez, who informed him that he had just purchased fifty acres of land from a Mr. Wong. John grimaced. "I wanted to buy that property five years ago, but Mr. Wong turned me down cold!" John explained.

"I'll sell it to you!"

"You will?" John was amazed. He remembered how he had claimed that property by faith the day Wong had turned him down.

"Sí! I will sell it to you today—right this moment!"

"Okay." John grinned. "Let's go to Turner's Restaurant and discuss the details!"

Within ten minutes, the two men had agreed on the price of eight thousand dollars for the property: two thousand to be paid within thirty days, and the remaining balance within ninety days thereafter. John shook his friend's hand, and the deal was closed.

He jogged the five blocks home to tell Josie about the land acquisition. "I just bought fifty acres of beautiful farmland right along the highway for eight thousand dollars!"

"That's nice," she replied. "Do you have the money?"

"Of course not. If God wants us to have it, the financing is His business."

That night, John called Pastor Sattler, who was already in bed, deep in slumber. John woke him up with his opening broadside: "Pastor Sattler, this is Brother John in Victoria, Mexico. I've just called to tell you that I've found a piece of property for sale and have made a deal to buy it!" John filled him in on the details, then waited for his response. But it was less than enthusiastic.

"Great. What are you going to do for money?"

"I don't have any at the present time, but I have twenty-nine days before I need it!"

"Then what did you call me for?" Sattler was still negative.

"Well, you challenged me to 'step out on faith.' Now I want to know about your faith." For a moment, it was completely silent, and John wondered if he had spoken too strongly.

"Well," Sattler finally replied, "that's not exactly what I had in mind when we were talking about stepping out on faith. Fifty acres and eight thousand dollars when you're dead broke is quite a step—a giant step!"

John couldn't argue with that. When the conversation ended a few moments later, he had no idea what his challenge had meant to the Louisiana cleric.

At the end of twenty-nine days, John had no money—absolutely none. Mr. Rodriguez would want two thousand dollars tomorrow morning. John wondered why God always seemed to wait until the last five minutes to make His move. The sun set, and darkness settled over Victoria. John waited in the deep silence of his home for the miracle that *had* to happen.

At ten o'clock, the phone rang. Pastor Sattler was on the line. After a brief exchange of greetings, he got right to the point. "Brother John, you know when we want a new car or house we go to the bank and borrow money. I told the men in my church about the opportunity to buy those fifty acres, and seven of us went down to the bank and signed a personal note. You can get started on your land deal right now!"

"You mean you borrowed two thousand dollars?" John shouted.

"Oh no, Brother John, you misunderstood me. We signed a note for eight thousand dollars! The farm is yours! We're just saying that we love God and His work as much as we love things for ourselves."

John was almost jumping for joy. When he hung up the phone, he and Josie did a victory dance together around the room. John said, "All we need to do to sustain the Bible school from now on is to plant crops!"

John had been a lifeguard but never a farmer. He found a Mexican who owned a tractor and tried to hire him to plow his acreage. The tractor owner was eager for work but was also an honest man. "With all due respect to you, Mr. Eils, it's a waste of time and money to plow this ground. The earth is too dry. Corn will not grow in this dry, parched soil. No one else in this whole area is plowing. Are you sure you want me to do this job now?"

"Yes, I'm sure," John replied. "This is God's farm. The crop is His, the profit will be His, and the Bible school that will run because of it is His. If He wants to kill His crop, that's His business. All I have to do is put it in the ground, and then it's up to Him after that."

The man didn't argue further. While he was obediently plowing, an American friend who was living in Victoria came to the farm and confirmed the Mexican's opinion of John's judgment.

"John, you're a nice guy, but you're insane—absolutely insane. Planting a crop in this dry dust is a complete waste. You're just throwing your money away!"

"We'll see," John said with a smile.

The planting was finished at 5:00 p.m. on Saturday. At 5:15, torrential rains bathed the fifty acres of dust with the seed of faith. John and Josie drove out that night as the rains fell, and watched the Master Gardener water His fifty acres. God had purchased a farm; He was now watering it so it would produce.

The first harvest yielded twenty-two tons of shelled corn—which was sold for tremendous profit, since John was the only one in the area who had done any planting. The money from the crop alone covered the expenses of the Bible school for several months.

SEVENTEEN

"GOD" AND "LITTLE GOD"

The student population of the Nest of the Eagles was almost entirely made up of boys, except for two girls, Lola and Anita, who were housed in a home on school property. The men stayed in a dormitory that had been built by 125 hardworking Christians in Victoria.

Although John was happy with the way God was blessing the school, he wasn't surprised when a strange turn of events brought heavy clouds of suspicion over it. Scandal wasn't anything new in his ministry.

It all began when a bizarre and almost unbelievable tragedy took place at Villa Gran, a small village sixty miles north of Victoria. Although this event was totally unrelated to John's knowledge or ministry, it almost ended his work in Mexico.

The incident began when two brothers and a seventeen-year-old prostitute came out of the mountains and proclaimed to everyone in Villa Gran that they were gods.

The elder brother called himself "God," the younger dubbed himself "Little God," and the girl claimed she was a prophetess.

"God" demanded that the people of the village pay him tithes in return for the material prosperity he would give them. In their ignorance and superstition, they obeyed. When the material benefits didn't materialize, however, the people soon rebelled by refusing to pay the tithes.

To quell the rising tide of resentment, "God" went into a deep trance one afternoon in the center of the village. While the superstitious Mexicans surrounded him, he began sharing a "revelation" about a nearby cave, telling them that it contained enough treasure to make everyone rich for life.

Before he had spoken the last word, every Mexican within earshot was scrambling for a shovel, a pick, an ax—anything that could be used to dig. Then the race for the cave was on. Gold fever had reached epidemic proportions in Villa Gran.

After digging hysterically for most of the day and finding absolutely nothing, the villagers began doubting "God's" word. They demanded to know where the treasure had been hidden, and by their tone, "God" realized his very life was in danger. What happened next was hard to believe.

"It's here," the impostor told them. "The treasure is here. But there is something you must do to please the spirit world before you are going to find it."

"What do we need to do?" the villagers asked.

"You must find a human sacrifice to please the spirit world!"

The hysterical villagers grabbed a twenty-five-year-old woman and cut her heart out on the spot. Then, at "God's" orders, they threw her heart into the air as her body fell, lifeless, to the ground.

Having pleased the "spirit world," they resumed their search with renewed frenzy. Again, they found nothing! Anticipating another wave of rebellion, "God" demanded another human sacrifice to placate the spirit world. The greedy Mexicans grabbed a pregnant twenty-two-year-old woman and methodically cut her heart out with machetes.

The work continued, but still nothing was found. Slowly, the truth dawned on the villagers: "God" was a fraud. Realizing they were guilty of murder, the villagers buried the two bodies and swore everyone to secrecy. They knew that if the rurales discovered the matter, the ones responsible for the murder would be shot on the spot.

The secret stayed contained in the village for less than twenty-four hours. The first villagers who went to town compulsively talked about the "treasure hunt" in the strictest of confidence, and within minutes, the news was all over town—even reaching police headquarters.

The federal police, summoned from Mexico City, invaded the village of Villa Gran to arrest "God" and "Little God" and the "prophetess." When the police entered the village, "God" began shooting at them with a high-powered rifle. A federal inspector and two policemen were killed in the gun battle. "God" was shot, and "Little God" and the "prophetess" were captured and taken to Victoria, where they were jailed and charged with murder. Under interrogation, the "prophetess" said that they were religious missionaries who received their financial support from the United States.

John read the horrifying account of the "treasure hunt" in the newspaper, completely unaware of the far-reaching consequences it would have on him and his ministry. While the infamous pair from Villa Gran was awaiting trial in the Victorian jail, a scandal only slightly less sensational was brewing in John's Bible school, right under his unsuspecting nose.

Lola, one of the two female students, fell in love with a male student named Carlos Gonzalez. Carlos did not return her love, and his rejection made her both resentful and furious. One way or another, she intended to marry him.

Pastor Pancho, who lived on the school campus, came to John one afternoon in deep distress. "Brother John—oh, Brother John! We're in serious trouble!" Pancho shook his head and threw his hands in the air.

"What's the matter?"

"Lola has come to me with the alarming news that Carlos forced himself on her, and she demands that he marry her right now!"

Aware of the Mexicans' tendencies toward jealousy and their prizing of honor, John realized that there was trouble ahead, even if Lola's story turned out to be false. Just how much trouble, he didn't know. Unable to find Carlos, who had fled to his people in the mountains, John went to Lola's parents. Trying to calm the enraged father was like trying to lasso a wild steer with a rotted rope. John finally said, "Let me go to the boy's father and see what I can do. Will you give me twelve hours?"

"All right," Lola's father conceded. "You've got twelve hours, but that's all!"

In the tiny mountain village where Carlos lived, John found the terrified young man at his father's home. When he saw him, he got straight to the point: "Carlos, you know what Lola has accused you of. Is it true? Did you do this?"

"I didn't do it, Brother John," Carlos insisted. "I don't even like that girl—I never have. She wants me to marry her, and when I refused, she came up with this scheme to get her father to force me to marry her."

"Carlos, let me talk to your father. Where is he?"

"In the house. Please, come in!"

After John and Carlos had both explained the situation to his father in some detail, the old man—in spite of his mounting anger—agreed to come with John to Victoria and try to talk reason into Lola's father.

When John and Mr. Gonzalez arrived in Victoria, they found Pastor Pancho waiting for them at John's home in a state of semi-hysteria.

"Brother John! Oh, Brother John!" he cried, tugging at John's sleeve. "We've got to leave town, quick—right now! Hurry, hurry! We must leave!"

"Calm down, Pancho, and tell me what's happened since I left!"

"The girl's father didn't wait twelve hours. He went straight to the police right after you left. Look at this newspaper headline."

As John read the bold, black print, a wave of horror swept over him. It said, "Girl Raped in Protestant Church." The detailed story beneath that lurid headline named John's church in Victoria as the scene of the "rape." Having had some experience with the administration of justice in Mexico, John knew that everyone connected with the church or the school would be picked up, questioned, and perhaps imprisoned for years. With the newspaper in hand, he charged into the house and ordered Josie to pack her suitcase immediately.

"Why should I pack my suitcase?" Josie wanted to know.

"You're going to Monterrey for a while. Look at this newspaper!"

Josie glanced at the headline and then started packing. Experience had taught them that, if John were arrested, she could help only if she were outside where she could obtain money and approach friends for assistance. Money and "connections" are both important playing cards in the Mexican justice system.

Fifteen minutes later, Josie was on her way to Monterrey. She and John had agreed to communicate only by telegram in order to make it more difficult for the police to learn of her whereabouts.

When John and Mr. Gonzalez went to see Lola's father, he refused to talk to them. Instead, he sent word that he had hired an attorney and would take the church, the Bible school, the native pastors, and John to court for public trial.

The next morning, the newspaper featured this headline: "Church Used as House of Prostitution." This time, John was identified as the proprietor of the church. As soon as he read the article, he made two decisions: first, to go on a fast; second, to hire a lawyer—the best he could find. His very life was on the line, not to mention his ministry.

John located the finest criminal lawyer in Victoria and showed him the newspaper. The lawyer shoved it back. He had already seen it. Everyone had seen it. Today was a bonanza for newsboys in Victoria. All papers had been sold immediately.

The lawyer leaned back in his large swivel chair and propped his feet on his desk and. "Señor Eils, you are in a very tough spot. You know, the Mexican people are very jealous by nature. The public is on the girl's side right now. Regardless of her story's authenticity, she is the favorite at this moment. It will take a miracle to get you out of this one, Señor Eils—a real miracle!"

"Miracles are possible," John replied.

"For your sake, amigo, they had better be! You need one—a big one! I'll do the best I can for you, but I can't promise a thing."

When John left the lawyer's office, he felt nauseated. No matter how great his apprehension, however, he knew he had to visit Pancho and give him a word of encouragement. He had an sense that Pancho was ready to skip town," and he really couldn't blame him.

In Mexico, there is no trial by jury; a judge hears the case, and he alone decides the verdict and determines the sentence. If he's had a bad day and you have a bad lawyer, you can lose fifteen years of your life in ten minutes. John knew why Pancho wanted to run, but he also knew that the public and the police would see any effort to escape as a sign of guilt.

Finding the terrified pastor at his home, John gave him a pep talk. "Listen to me, Pancho! Whatever you do, don't run away!

That's all the authorities would need to put us all in federal prison in the morning. We're going to fight, because we're completely innocent!"

"Yes, I know, but who is going to believe us? Look at what the papers are saying! How are we going to prove to a judge that we're innocent?" John had no answers for these questions, and Pancho knew it.

As he left Pancho's house, John's parting words were, "If the police come after you, have your wife contact me quickly!"

That night at seven, there was a banging on John's front door. Expecting to find the police there to arrest him, John opened the door to find Pancho standing there sobbing, his fists flailing in the air.

"What's happened, Pancho? What on earth has happened?"

"We're ruined, John! We're ruined forever. We'll all be sent to prison for sure!"

"Pancho, get ahold of yourself and tell me what's wrong! Please, Pancho! Be quiet and just tell me!" John had to yell to make himself heard over Pancho's wailing.

"This afternoon at four o'clock," Pancho sobbed hysterically, "the police came to my house and pounded on the front door to get all my neighbors' attention. When I went to the door, they dragged me into their police car!" He paused for another outburst of sobs.

"Did they take you to jail and press charges?" John asked.

"No, no! Much worse than that! They took me to the red-light district and got the town's best-known prostitute and put her in the backseat with me!"

"Then what happened?"

"The police drove around and around the plaza very slowly, so that everyone could see me with that woman. All of Victoria was at the plaza today reading the newspapers about our church being a house of prostitution, and the police paraded me around the whole town with that prostitute! Brother John, no one will ever believe we are innocent!"

"What did they do then?" John asked mechanically. His mind was spinning.

"After everyone had seen us many times, they drove her back to the red-light district and dropped me off at my house. The damage is done. We're through."

"It looks very bad, that's true. But we're not running, Pancho. We're not finished yet—not by a long shot!"

With those words, John left the house abruptly and walked the mile to the massive, four-story jail and courthouse. He told the policeman in charge that he wanted to make a voluntary statement to a court reporter for the official court record. Although the judge welcomed a statement, one serious problem developed: The court reporter refused to record any facts that might indicate John's innocence. She chronicled only those which would point toward his guilt. John protested—politely at first, then vehemently. The policeman in charge slowly shrugged his shoulders and arched his eyebrows, as if to indicate that he was helpless to correct the injustice John wasn't supposed to notice.

Suddenly, John was struck by an inspiration. He stood to his feet and demanded a federal investigation. The policeman was shocked, but, by law, he was forced to grant his request.

Feeling some sense of relief, John attempted to leave the courthouse, but a short, stocky Mexican stepped right in front of him. John waited while the man's dark, piercing eyes slowly looked him over several times. Finally, the Mexican spoke, softly and with complete authority.

"Gringo, do you know what you've done by asking for a federal trial?"

"I think so, but you tell me."

"If you lose, the minimum sentence is ten years in the federal prison. I repeat: ten years!"

"I'm innocent. I have nothing to worry about!" John bravely protested.

"You'd better be innocent, amigo, you better be."

"Why are you so interested in my case?" John asked.

"Let me tell you who I am," the man hissed, flashing a federal inspector's badge. "I am with the federal government, here to investigate the 'God' and 'Little God' matter! Does that sound familiar to you, amigo?"

The inspector's eyes were boring through him as if he could see into his very soul. John didn't flinch but unblinkingly returned the cold stare.

The inspector continued, "The young 'prophetess' captured with 'Little God' told me she was getting support from America to carry out her 'religious' work in Mexico. You also get support from America for your religious work. I think you're connected with them, and I will leave no stone unturned to prove your guilt."

John again tried to leave, but the federal inspector didn't budge. He obviously had more to say.

"You wanted to know why I'm so interested in your case, so I'm going to tell you. The inspector that was murdered by 'God' when we invaded the village of Villa Gran was my best friend. I've sworn on his grave to track down every person connected in any way with his death and to send him to prison for life. If I can find one small shred, just one tiny bit, of evidence against you, señor, you will never—absolutely never—get out of prison." The inspector left without another word.

EIGHTEEN

THE TRIAL

Close to despair, John went back to his dark, empty house. The phone was ringing when he opened the door. He hurriedly picked up the receiver and heard the welcome voice of David Coote. Never one to waste words, Coote opened the conversation with "John, what in the world is going on down there? I've been getting calls from all over America—something about you running a house of prostitution. What's the story?"

John explained in some detail everything that had happened—from "God" and "Little God" to the events that had happened that afternoon. When he finished, he waited anxiously for his friend's reaction. It came instantly and forcefully.

"John, I want you to get the finest lawyer money can hire. I'll support you to the limit—and then some. If it costs ten thousand dollars, that's fine. Give this fight everything you've got. Every student on campus will pray daily until this crisis has ended. God be with you—and win this one, John! Win it, whatever the cost!"

John hung up the receiver and breathed a prayer of thanks for the timely phone call and the total support from such a wise and influential friend. He wondered how many of his supporters in the States would react like President Coote had. When he came through this ordeal, he would know without a single doubt who his real friends were.

Still sitting in the dark by the telephone, John thought of Josie and what she was doing at this moment. Like him, she was waiting and hoping and fearing, knowing that the next few days could wipe out all their efforts over the past eight years and all their dreams and plans for the future. Her husband's freedom—perhaps his very life—teetered in the balance.

As John walked from the phone to his bed, he breathed a prayer for God's help. He didn't eat dinner, since he had started fasting in preparation for the trial, which had been set for the following week.

The words of Jesus from Luke 12:11–12 soothed his tortured mind as he drifted toward sleep: *"And when they bring you unto the…magistrates, and powers, take ye no thought how or what thing ye shall answer, or what ye shall say: for the Holy Ghost shall teach you in the same hour what ye ought to say."*

Just before falling asleep, John made up his mind that he would not rehearse his testimony, though he was tempted to do so. He would simply place his ministry and his life in the hands of God, and trust His promises.

On the morning of the trial, John telegrammed Josie. *Not in the lion's den yet but can hear them roaring.* Then he left his home and headed for the courthouse, lost in thought. In a few hours, it would all be over. The cards were stacked against him. Unless the miracle his lawyer had talked about became a reality today, he could expect to spend at least ten years in federal prison.

Entering the large, rectangular courtroom where the trial was to be held, he sat down beside his attorney, who was thumbing through his court-recorded statements and reviewing his line of defense. Many newsmen were there, waiting in anticipation for a story that would feed the scandal-loving souls in the plaza.

Photographers lined the wall, checking and rechecking their equipment. They did not want to miss the facial expressions of shock and shame that would surely follow the sentencing. The federal inspector paced back and forth like a caged lion awaiting its next meal of raw flesh. This was John's day of doom. If ever he needed a miracle from God, it was now.

The whole courtroom snapped to attention as the portly, black-robed judge strode to his lofty seat and smashed his gavel on the oak desk in front of him. Everyone was ordered to stand while the judge gave a brief, oversimplified explanation of the basic issues involved in the trial. When he had finished, all were seated, and the action began. Lola was called to the stand.

Under the lawyers' examination and cross-examination, she insisted that Carlos Gonzalez had forced himself upon her and that she had been held at the Bible school against her will and forced into prostitution. Upon counsel's request that she point out the man responsible for her captivity, she directed her finger toward John. When Lola stated that Anita, the other girl at the Bible school, was also a prostitute, Anita's parents stood up, loudly protesting their daughter's innocence and pleading with the reporters not to print the monstrous lie.

Lola's parents stood next and defended their daughter's truthfulness. Accusations and counter-accusations flew back and forth. The judge nearly splintered his gavel before he was able to restore a semblance of order in the courtroom. Then he announced that the veracity of Lola's charges would be determined by a physical examination of both girls immediately by a local physician.

Both sets of parents jumped again to their feet, protesting loudly, but their arguments fell on deaf ears. The judge ordered a recess until one o'clock, at which time the physician's findings would be revealed.

The hours dragged on. The spectators and reporters, afraid to give up their seats, stayed in the courtroom to await the next development in this sensational case. John paced back and forth and stared, unseeing, at the floor. The stalky federal inspector didn't leave the courtroom for one minute. He stood like a stone statue, his arms crossed over his barrel chest, his hawklike eyes following John as if searching for some movement that would betray his guilt.

As the afternoon sun bathed the courtroom in warmth, some of the spectators—long accustomed to a daily siesta—started drowse and nod off. The pounding of the judge's gavel woke them with a start. The tension in the courtroom mounted to an almost unbearable level as the judge sat reading the physician's report in silence.

John's hands were suddenly wet with perspiration, and he fought the nausea that threatened to overtake him. That piece of paper the judge was studying so intently was either his ticket to freedom or his sentence to ten years in federal prison. If the physician had reported that both girls were virgins, he was free. If not, he would be sent to prison.

John folded his clammy hands between his knees and lowered his head. Almost aloud, he whispered, "O God, be near me!"

Reporters' pens were poised over their notebooks; photographers adjusted their lenses for the perfect shot just moments away. The whole courtroom, the whole state of Tamaulipas—surely the hosts of heaven itself—were anxiously awaiting the verdict.

After adjusting his horn-rimmed spectacles and vigorously clearing his throat, the judge said, "The physician's report declares that the girl Lola is not in a state of moral purity—"

Reporters' pens went flying as the courtroom broke into an uproar. The gringo missionary was guilty! This was the proof!

The judge's pounding gavel restored order, and his booming voice demanded that he be allowed to finish his statement: "The physician's report declares that the girl Lola is not in a state of moral purity but that she has not been in contact with a man for at least the last six months."

A mountain fell off John's shoulders. So great was his sense of relief that he was oblivious to the pandemonium in the courtroom—the flashbulbs popping like popcorn, the judge's gavel pounding repeatedly on the desk, trying in vain to quell the turmoil.

Lola was crying convulsively now, and her father was white with terror. Señor Eils would surely have him sent to jail because of his false accusations! The face of the federal inspector wore a mask of gloom and disappointment.

"Please! Please, be quiet until the court is adjourned. There's more to report!" the judge declared in his commanding voice. The noise gradually subsided as he continued. "The other girl, Anita, is, beyond all medical doubt, a pure and chaste virgin."

Sighs and sobs broke out anew, and Anita's parents wept with joy. The gavel cracked again, and the judge said at last, "The accused man, Señor John Eils, is found by this court to be completely innocent. In addition, all the people connected with his religious ministry are also cleared of all charges. Case dismissed!"

Reporters scrambled for the door, while the remainder of the spectators gathered in little groups to discuss the astounding outcome of the case. John's attorney shook his head. "You got your miracle!" The barrister beamed. "God has rescued you from a terrible fate! Do you want to press charges against Lola's father?"

"No, indeed! I've had my day in court, and I hope I'll never have another one!" John's heart was so full of joy and gratitude to God that there was no room in it for rancor and bitterness. He was only glad that God's triumphant gospel would continue to be preached in that area. Nothing is impossible with God—not even in Mexico!

John nearly floated down the hall toward the telegraph office. Josie—poor Josie—would be waiting in agony.

The telegram was delivered to her in Monterrey an hour later. With trembling hands, she opened the yellow envelope and read, *Daniel is out of the lion's den. Come home.*

The scandal was over. John and Josie Eils were again free to serve God.

EPILOGUE

1972

John Eils has now become a Mexican citizen, and his ministry in Victoria still thrives. John and Josie have recently been joined by Sam and Jackie Cooksey, originally from Modesto. The Cookseys are being marvelously used to direct the Bible school, where enrollment is close to fifty students, and the mission churches.

In 1972, Ercel and Cathy Lewis also joined the team. Ercel, who studied agriculture at Texas Tech University, is the farm administrator. The Holy Spirit is working through these three couples to produce a mighty revival in Mexico.

At the writing of this book, the local authorities of Victoria had recently asked John to open an orphanage. An opportunity now exists for John to purchase an ex-governor's mansion and ninety-two acres of land for $160,000 to be used as a haven for homeless Mexican children.

Along with meeting the continually multiplying challenges of Mexico, John and Josie are also striving to reach other

Spanish-speaking peoples beyond Mexico's borders. John has established a radio ministry in Colombia and is helping finance a Bible school there, which was started by Don Gwinn, another graduate of IBC. A radio ministry is also being planned for Ecuador.

What makes a ministry like this possible? It is the loving concern of people like Pastor Herb Sweat of Washington, Pennsylvania, who is an old friend of the Eilses and has faithfully stood behind their ministry for many years. True to his vow, John has never begged for funds for his ministry; but as he has traveled from place to place, explaining his ministry, God has laid it upon the hearts of many people, like Pastor Sweat, to pledge support to this work.

ABOUT THE AUTHOR

Pastor John C. Hagee is founder and senior pastor of Cornerstone Church in San Antonio, Texas, as well as the founder and president of John Hagee Ministries, which broadcasts his radio and television teachings across the United States and 249 nations worldwide.

He received his theological training from Southwestern Assemblies of God University, his bachelor of arts degree from Trinity University in San Antonio, Texas, and his master's degree from North Texas University.

Pastor John has given millions of dollars toward humanitarian causes in Israel. In 2006, he founded Christians United for Israel, a grassroots association that promotes support for Israel and gives voice to many pro-Israeli ministries and organizations. Pastor John is also the author of thirty-three books, including four *New York Times* best sellers.